ARE YOU TIRED?

by *Frances Hunter*

Published by
HUNTER BOOKS
City of Light
201 McClellan Road
Kingwood, Texas 77339, U.S.A

BOOKS BY CHARLES ♥ FRANCES HUNTER

A CONFESSION A DAY KEEPS THE DEVIL AWAY
ANGELS ON ASSIGNMENT
ARE YOU TIRED?
BORN AGAIN! WHAT DO YOU MEAN?
COME ALIVE
DON'T LIMIT GOD
FOLLOW ME
GOD IS FABULOUS
GOD'S ANSWER TO FAT...LOØSE IT!
GOD'S CONDITIONS FOR PROSPERITY
HANDBOOK FOR HEALING
HIS POWER THROUGH YOU
HOT LINE TO HEAVEN
HOW TO HEAL THE SICK
HOW TO MAKE YOUR MARRIAGE EXCITING
IF YOU REALLY LOVE ME...
IMPOSSIBLE MIRACLES
IT'S SO SIMPLE (formerly HANG LOOSE WITH JESUS)
LET'S GO WITNESSING (formerly GO, MAN, GO)
MEMORIZING MADE EASY
MY LOVE AFFAIR WITH CHARLES
NUGGETS OF TRUTH
POSSESSING THE MIND OF CHRIST
P.T.L.A. (Praise the Lord, Anyway!)
SIMPLE AS A.B.C.
SINCE JESUS PASSED BY
the fabulous SKINNIE MINNIE RECIPE BOOK
SUPERNATURAL HORIZONS (from Glory to Glory)
THE DEVIL WANTS YOUR MIND
THE TWO SIDES OF A COIN
THIS WAY UP!
WHY SHOULD "I" SPEAK IN TONGUES?

ISBN 0-917726-65-0

TABLE OF CONTENTS

For information about the City
of Light Video teaching tapes,
audio tapes, price list of Hunter
Books, write to:

HUNTER BOOKS
City of Light
201 McClellan Road
Kingwood, Texas 77339, U.S.A

In the event your Christian Bookstore does
not have any of the books written by Charles
and Frances Hunter or published by Hunter
Books, please write for price list and order
form from HUNTER BOOKS.

CHAPTER ONE

WHAT IS HAPPENING TO ME?

Get a comfortable chair and sit down, because you won't put this book down until you have completely finished reading it!

God has given me a message to share with the Body of Christ which can save your life!

When you saw the title of this book ARE YOU TIRED?, you may have thought, "Tired of what?" It could mean:

"Are you tired of not having enough money?"
"Are you tired of going to church?"
"Are you tired of being sick?"
"Are you tired of problems?"
"Are you tired of being depressed?"

or it could mean a number of different things. However, in the simple title, I asked you an honest question with no strings attached.

Are you physically tired?

Have you been experiencing an energy lag?

Are you dragging yourself around much more than you used to do?

Do you have difficulty remembering things you should know?

Do you have spells when reading the Bible isn't as exciting as it used to be?

Do you have difficulty making decisions which are simple?

Are you forgetful?

In spite of the exhaustion you feel, do you have difficulty going to sleep at nights?

Is your sleep restless at times?

During the last two years I could have honestly answered "Yes" to each and every one of those questions, but how I praise God that today I can honestly answer each one of them with an unqualified "No!"

For someone who has always had such a positive confession where the Word of God is concerned, it may seem that I am making a very negative confession. My total honesty is with the hope in mind that the things I am sharing with you in this book will not have to happen to you.

During the last two years, I have gone through the most difficult time I have ever had in my entire life. As I look back right now, it all seems like a nightmare which sneaked up on me and I didn't even realize what was happening. Had it not been for the tender loving mercy of God and His grace, I would be dead right now!

Probably the only one who really knew about it was Charles because he lives with me and he saw what was happening even though he could do nothing about it.

I want to share my problems with you so that the same thing does not happen to you!

I am one of those individuals who has been blessed all of my life with a tremendous amount of energy. Not only do I have a natural reserve of energy, it seems as though I also have a tremendous source of adrenalin which enables me to force and to push myself above and beyond what I ought to push. That's a blessing at times, but I also discovered that it is not such a blessing at other times because you keep pushing beyond the normal and intelligent limits which can cause an individual to run into some real problems.

I hardly remember when this all started because I always ignore any little symptoms the devil tries to put on me. But somewhere along the line during the last five years I began to notice little changes which seemed unimportant in the beginning. Nothing big, but little warning signals began to occur.

It seemed to me that I could not accomplish as much work as I formerly did. Since I have always been a terrific "work horse", what might seem a slow-down to me might not seem that way to someone else. There were little warning signals which I didn't even recognize and instead I attempted to ignore some radical changes that were occurring in my body.

I began to notice an unusual desire for sweets. I began to notice that even though I would be extremely tired when I went to bed, I would have diffi-

culty going to sleep, and my sleep seemed to be a
restless sleep with a lot of tossing and turning during the night interspersed with periods of wakeful-
ness.

If I tried to get up, I would realize how
exhausted I was. I would climb right back in bed
and then be wide awake again! The room never
seemed to be the right temperature—either my feet
were cold or I was perspiring around the neck. We
never seemed to be able to set the thermostat correctly so that I would be comfortable enough to go
right to sleep. It was turn and toss night after night,
regardless of whether we were at home or in a motel
on the road.

One night as we were working in our office at
home, I had a lot of projects to finish before going to
bed and it seemed as if my energy just completely
disappeared. I don't remember ever having such a
desire in my entire life to just go to bed and go to
sleep immediately. Because I knew I had to finish
my job, I ran out to the kitchen and made a pot of
strong coffee, drank two cups and ate a dish of ice
cream with hot fudge sauce for energy. As I returned
to my desk, I thought I would collapse because I was
so tired.

That certainly seemed peculiar to me because
the caffeine in coffee and the sugar in the ice cream
and hot fudge sauce should have kept anyone awake
for at least another couple of hours. I looked at
Charles and said, "Honey, do you think something is
wrong with me? I don't seem to be able to push myself the way I used to. Do you think it could possibly

be that I'm getting older and just won't be able to do the things I used to." We laughed and decided that maybe we were getting a little bit older and that maybe God didn't intend for us to always keep a sixteen-hour a day schedule as we had maintained.

Nothing could have kept me awake. I simply had to go to bed. Even with the coffee and sugar inside my body, I dropped off into a "dead" sleep this time.

Even though it was not a constant thing at that time, today I can look back and see that when I was working at night, it became more and more of a necessity to get some "extra" energy through coffee, Pepsi or a dish of ice cream. Looking back, the words, "Honey, I'm so tired!" seemed to become a regular part of my conversation with Charles. Even though we would comment on how often I said those words, we basically ignored them.

It seemed as though I was tired in the morning regardless of when I went to bed at night.

It seemed as though I was tired at noon regardless of how late I had stayed in bed in the morning.

It seemed as though I was tired at night regardless of whether or not I had taken a nap or had done little or a lot of work that day.

Soon it seemed as though I was exhausted all the time. A REAL WARNING SIGNAL.

I love being in the ministry. I love each and every one of our speaking dates. I love writing the monthly letters to those who are a part of our ministry. I love writing the tabloid which we send out every three months. I love booking all of our speaking dates.

We are probably one of the few ministries in the world today who still personally do all the little things I have mentioned above. We do them all because we love doing them!

Looking back, I don't even remember when I began to lose my interest in doing my normal work in the ministry. It seemed the piles of letters I needed to answer grew bigger and bigger until they almost stifled me. I began to dislike dictating and had difficulty getting all the things said that I wanted to get across in a letter.

All of these things came so gradually and so stealthily upon me that neither of us realized what was happening. We didn't even seem to be aware that anything unusual was occurring.

I began to lose my usual enthusiasm and exhuberance for almost everything.

I wanted to be alone, and when I was alone, I wanted to go to bed and sleep.

I didn't want to have company and I didn't want to go anywhere.

I just wanted to go to sleep.

I was soooooooooooooo tired!

When I sat down in a chair, I didn't want to get up. It was too much effort because I WAS SO TIRED! My legs seemed to weigh a thousand pounds, and it was just too much effort to get up out of a chair. Once I had prepared dinner at home and put it on the table, I checked carefully to make sure I had not forgotten anything. It seemed that once I sat down, it was almost a physical impossibility for me to get up again.

From the glorious day when I was born again, I have been a fanatic about reading the Bible. I love to spend hours and hours reading and meditating in the Word. I love researching in the Bible when I'm going to teach a new subject or write a book. My disinterest in reading the Word came so slowly that I didn't even realize it had happened. For no reason that I could fathom, I suddenly found the Bible difficult to get into. The Bible had lost its zip! I would force myself to read the Word because I knew that I should. When I finished, I couldn't remember a single thing I had read. Has that ever happened to you?

People would come up to me in prayer lines and say they were exhausted all the time, and I would say, "Get into the Word of God—nothing will give you a quick pick-up physically and mentally faster than hearing from God." It had always worked for me in the past. Why was I having such a difficult time reading the Word and then not being able to understand what was going on?

Another little thing went wrong, and I ignored that, too. My two big toes had not had much feeling for years, but suddenly they felt completely dead. I would pray for my feet and when that didn't help, I decided it was because I was on them so much during services.

During this entire time, Charles and I prayed and prayed for me. We prayed for more strength, we confessed more strength, we spoke the Word over my body, and I could hardly wait for us to say

"Amen" before I would promptly go to bed.

Suddenly, a shocking fact became apparent to me. I didn't seem to be able to remember as well as I formerly did. It seemed I would start to quote a verse of scripture and after the first few words, I was unable to remember it correctly. Not only that, to know where it was located in the Bible was an absolute impossibility. It seemed as though even my favorite scriptures would elude my memory. If I finally got them quoted, they were slightly mixed up (at best)! Fear began to grip my mind. Was I getting sick with some kind of an unknown disease?

Maybe if I ate something it would give me energy. What should I eat?

Something to give me a fast pick-up.

A piece of chocolate? A candy bar?

A big tall glass of orange juice?

A dish of ice cream? Maybe a little chocolate sauce on top of it? Both are good for the energy. Maybe I ought to have three scoops of ice cream because I am so drained of energy. I'm exhausted. I'm worn out. "Something will give me energy." But nothing did! I just gained weight!

God, where are you? God, is something going wrong with me? God, I need a touch from you!

Charles and I both love to lay hands on the sick. If there is any ministry to which God has called us to, it is to lay hands on the sick. We go to service after service, night after night, and because we love to lay hands on the sick, we never go home until the last person who wants to have hands laid on them has an opportunity to be healed, delivered and set free regardless of the size of the audience or the time of night.

One night on the way to the motel after an especially long (and powerful) service, I said to Charles, "Honey, I am so tired I can't stand it!" At that particular moment I felt I couldn't ever lay hands on people again because I was so extremely exhausted. I felt as though it was draining my very life out of me.

Something else began to happen. During this period of extreme tiredness and exhaustion, we have seen the greatest increase in the healing ministry that we have ever enjoyed since we became Spirit-filled. We have seen many services where 85, 90 and even 95 per cent of the people who have come forward for healing have been totally healed and yet I have walked out of those services and said to Charles, "Honey, we've got to stop laying hands on everyone at all of our services because this is absolutely killing me!"

Both of us believe in divine health and we spoke healing and health plus energy to my body, but it wasn't working. You may wonder at what seems to be a very negative frame of mind, but I am being honest with you because I believe that this honesty is going to help you.

Charles has a compassion for the sick like no one I have ever known, seen or heard about. He cannot leave a meeting until he has done all he can to alleviate sickness, regardless of what it is. Sometimes I would almost wish he didn't have that much compassion because all I could think of was, "Charles,

I'm so exhausted I can hardly move!" Then we would go back to the motel and I could hardly get my clothes off before I literally collapsed in bed.

Many times Charles would remove my stockings and shoes because I would fall asleep before I could get them off.

In the meantime, my entire body felt sluggish and my legs seemed to weigh more and more all the time. I continued gaining a tremendous amount of weight. All the pounds I had lost when I wrote the book GOD'S ANSWER TO FAT started coming back and it seemed as though I was completely powerless and helpless to stop what was happening within my own body. At this point I didn't really care how much weight I gained because I was far more interested in feeling good again and that took precedence over everything else.

Then Charles and I began to have discussions about the fact that he could not stop praying for people until the last one was taken care of. I knew it was pushing me beyond my human limitations to stay up that long. We talked about having someone take me back to the motel when I became exhausted and Charles would come later. We could never do this because something inside of me made me stay, too, because of the compassion I have for the sick.

After the morning meetings, it was all I could do to crawl into the motel where I would go into a "dead" sleep until just before it was time for us to run to the evening service. There were nights and nights when it was absolute torture for me to get out of bed, get dressed and go to a miracle service. However, when I got to the service, I'd walk in that very special anointing that only God can give, and there was not a single, solitary person who would have ever suspected that anything was wrong with me!

Then a very unusual thing happened! We flew home one day after we had been on the road for approximately two weeks, and planned to go right to the office. The first thing I always want to do when we return from a trip is to go to the office directly from the airport, see all of our employees, share some of the miracles that happened on the trip, and get things going that needed to be done from the trip.

I had experienced a real miserable night's sleep (or lack of sleep), so when our plane landed around ten o'clock in the morning, I said to Charles, "Honey, would you mind taking me home? I don't feel up to going into the office right now, so I think I'll go home for an hour or two and take a nap. As soon as I wake up, then I'll go to the office. But right now, I'm just toooooo tired to do anything!"

Charles said, "All right," and took me home. He went into the office and told the staff not to call me because I was tired, but said, "As soon as she wakes up she'll come to the office."

I DIDN'T WAKE UP FOR 24 HOURS!

It was one of the most unusual "sleeps" I had ever had. When I finally woke up the next morning around ten o'clock, I had a feeling of having been drugged. I didn't wake up at all, not even when Charles got into bed. I remember trying to turn over in the bed during the night and thought the most

peculiar thing before I sailed right off to sleep again.
I thought, "My body is too heavy to turn over in
bed." My arms both felt like dead weights, and they
didn't have enough strength in them to turn me over
in bed, and I couldn't generate enough energy to
change from one side to the other, so I just laid
there! Struggle as I might, there just wasn't enough
energy to turn my body over.

The next day Charles said, "Honey, you must
have really been tired because you sure slept a long
time!"

I said, "Well, praise the Lord, I feel good today,
but I must have really been tired yesterday." I could
not believe that I had slept that long. It seemed impossible for me to believe that I could have actually
stayed in bed that long. We decided that I probably
just needed more sleep than he did, because some
people do require more sleep than others.

I began to notice that I also wanted to sleep later
in the mornings than I usually did. I had real difficulty getting myself going in the mornings, but
credited it to the fact that I was probably "working
too hard"!

Charles and I prayed without ceasing for a return of my energy, but it seemed we were calling
upon deaf ears, and yet we were seeing prayer after
prayer answered in other areas.

I continued to gain weight because of the com-
pelling desire to eat something sweet "to give me
energy." It was so overwhelming that I could do
nothing to stop it simply because my body was
screaming for something, and since I didn't know

what it was, I tried to give it some of the "energy foods which just weren't doing a single thing for me.

Maybe if we had come home from one trip, and I had slept for twenty-four hours, and it had never happened again, we could have ignored it. But, about a month after the first sleep binge we came home from another trip and as we were driving from the airport I said to Charles, "You'd better take me home again today, honey, because I'm exhausted and I need just a little sleep. Tell the office not to call me, and I'll check in as soon as I wake up."

I knew it was for just a little nap, but even so I put on my nightgown and went to bed. It felt so good I knew I would be up and full of energy quickly.

I SLEPT ANOTHER 24 HOURS.

I couldn't believe that I hadn't stirred for another twenty-four hour period, but I hadn't! What could possibly be the matter with me? Was I getting so old that I was just completely falling apart? I didn't believe that at all, because God has called me for a special work, and I know that Moses lived to be one hundred and twenty years old before he died, so I couldn't rationalize God letting me disintegrate.

Was I not eating properly? Charles and I are not "junk food" eaters, and our house is literally free of any of the usual "nibbling" foods that most people have around the house. We are salad, fresh vegetable and chicken eaters. When we are out, we eat a lot of fish because we love that, too. The only problem might have been the ice cream, but everybody knows that ice cream is good for you!

What could be causing this tremendous energy lag? Why did these tremendous energy lags come in "spells"? I began to notice a pattern had formed. I would go through a period of one or two weeks when I would have a real sag in my energy, and then for a week or two I would seemingly be over them, and I would think I had experienced the last one I would ever have, and then bang, another one would hit me!

During these "spells" as I began to call them, I noticed that I could not think as well as I normally did. It seemed to me that I was having a lapse of memory. I began to wonder what was happening to my brain. Someone would tell me a very simple thing at the office and I would think, "I didn't understand a thing they said."

We rebuked the devil. We bound Satan from entering our home and told him to take this exhaustion and run with it because we didn't want it any more, and then I'd have to go to bed because I was so tired.

The devil loves to have a field day with your mind. I began to wonder if I was getting senile. There are many kinds of thoughts the devil loves to put into your mind at a time like this. He reminded me of a disease which they call today Alzheimer's disease. This disease causes the loss of memory. I had laid hands on enough people with that disease to know that it is straight from the enemy. I rebuked even the thought of that disease.

CHAPTER TWO

HONEY, I'M SICK!

Finally, I had about reached the end of my rope. I said to Charles, "Honey, I think I had better go to the doctor. In spite of all our prayers and you laying hands on me ten to fifteen times a day, I seem to be getting worse." I even laughingly said to him, "Every time you pray, I seem to get worse!"

There were many times when we were scheduled to go on a trip and I was so exhausted that I would think I could not make it. And yet, every time we had to go, I would get up out of bed and get on the plane. We've never cancelled a single trip.

Let me ease your mind right now before you begin to ask yourself why a faith-filled person would ever go to a doctor. I do not have any hangups about going to a doctor. We always go to God first, but if we don't get healed, I give thanks for the Spirit-filled physician to whom I can go. Sometimes Christians get some real pseudo faith and think they

would be backsliding if they went to a doctor. I have
known many people who stood on their "faith" and
refused to go to doctors. They had beautiful funer-
als! Faith always needs to be tempered with common sense.

God has healed me of many things, but there are
times for some reason or other when I have not been
able to connect and receive a healing. I have never
had a moment of guilt in going to a doctor.

I suffered agony with an open ulcer on my leg
for over seven years. I believed that God would heal
it, and He did! But only after I went to the hospital
and had it debrided! Then the healing was supernatural because they told me I would have to be on
bedrest for months. On the eighth day, I was up and
out of bed because God had done such a wonderful
job! All of the physicians and staff of our local hospital were amazed because of the unbelievably fast
healing. I gave all the glory to God!

After discussing my tiredness at length, Charles
decided to go to the doctor with me and we both got
a surprise. The first thing the doctor did was the
usual blood pressure check. Since God gave me a
new heart ten years ago, my blood pressure has been
normal. The readings were now elevated. I could not
understand this change in my pressure because
when God heals you, He HEALS you! What caused
my blood pressure to go up?

I described my "tiredness" to the doctor and
mentioned the fact that it seemed to me that it usually came in "spells" during which time I would
sleep for unusually long periods of time and then for

a short time I would seemingly recover from whatever my problem was.

The doctor questioned me about my activities and about our work. Then he kiddingly said, "Frances, you're getting older and you've just got to learn to slow down." He continued the examination and added, "You have to remember when you get to your age you just have to take it a little easier than you do. You keep thinking you're a young person running all over the United States and all over the world as well. You're just not up to it like you were when you were ten years younger."

I commented, "I don't believe that's it because I seem to be basically normal until I get one of these 'spells' and then I literally fall apart."

He said, "Let me give you a shot of B-12 and see if that doesn't perk you up." He gave me the shot and he was right—it did "perk" me up—for about twenty-four hours. Then—there I was again sleeping around the clock!

We went on our next trip and I said to Charles, "It seems to me that every time I turn around I get one of these 'spells'." (I couldn't think of anything else to call them and I remembered somewhere back in my childhood about old ladies having 'spells'.) I continued, "This can't be happening to a Christian, but do you think I'm getting old enough that I'm just having 'old lady' spells or something like that?"

Then I decided there was no way I could have "spells". But what was it I had? I could not figure it out.

I'm being real "nitty-gritty" when I tell you that

I got to a point where I could not force myself to read the Bible when I was in one of those periods of exhaustion. Try as I might, there was no way my mind could force my body to read. Even if I desperately tried, nothing registered in my mind. Right in the middle of reading, I would fall sound asleep!

One day we were coming home from a road trip and I was so worn down I thought I wasn't going to make it home. When we finally did reach Houston, I said to Charles, "Honey, take me home right now because I'm falling asleep on my feet. I've got to have a nap before I go into the office."

He took me home. I started taking my clothes off as soon as I hit the front door. I almost ran into our bedroom because I was actually wondering if I could stay awake until I reached the bed.

"Charles, get me something to give me some energy. I can't stand this tired feeling. Fix me some hot chocolate or some ice cream so I can have a quick pick-up."

My body was screaming from being pushed beyond what it could do and nothing seemed to be getting better, just worse and worse.

Charles brought me something sweet. It didn't make any difference if it was peanut butter and jelly or ice cream with chocolate sauce, my body was screaming for something sweet. I would eat whatever he brought (if I could stay awake that long) and then right back to sleep I would go. It was almost as though I was drugged.

What little flashes of alertness I did have were spent wondering if I had some horrible disease from which I was going to die. Those are some of the most terrifying moments an individual can ever have because you're too exhausted to fight off the darts of the devil. My head would swim before I fell into a deep sleep.

My eyes would open. Was that the telephone ringing? Let it ring, I can't answer it. I'm just too tired to talk to anyone. I think I'll turn over in bed. No, I'm too tired. I think I'll just lay right here. Oh, no, here comes that horrible blackness again. "Oh, God, I'm your child, touch me, touch me. I need help!" And I slid down into the abyss where I knew nothing mattered anyway.

THIS TIME I SLEPT FOR 48 HOURS right around the clock! Charles would try to rouse me and encourage me to get up and eat something to "give me strength." He thought if I walked around outside in the yard, it would make me feel better. I thought that walking in the yard was about the most revolting thing I could think of! "Oh, God, let me go back to sleep!"

Charles would try to get me up at mealtime and encouraged me to come to the table to eat. I vaguely remember trying to do this, but before I took two or three bites, I fell asleep again. Charles had to lead me back to the bedroom. With the minute amount of alertness I had, I said, "Charles, bring me the rest of the dish of ice cream. Maybe if I can just eat a little of that, I'll get some energy."

Bless his heart, Charles would even feed me the ice cream, waking me up between each bite, but nothing did any good.

And I continued to gain weight.

Charles would say, "Honey, I know how you feel about gaining weight. Why don't you go back on the foods you talked about in GOD'S ANSWER TO FAT. You know that always works!"

I couldn't do it. My body seemed to be crying for something sweet. I felt almost like a dope addict. There was no satisfaction until I got something in my mouth that was super sweet. Even that didn't satisfy except momentarily because I would go right back to sleep.

I decided to go back to the doctor when I got over this "spell". I did, and he took a blood test and decided I needed a little thyroid because the levels were slightly low. He prescribed a very small dose of thyroid to pick me up and give me some energy. This shocked me because when I was saved in 1965 God healed me of Addison's disease. I was taking nineteen grains of thyroid every single day because my thyroid had been completely destroyed.

I forgot all about taking thyroid after I got saved because God had supernaturally healed me and totally restored my thyroid. It has remained normal ever since then.

Let me repeat a previous statement I made. God doesn't heal you to let you get sick again, so this sudden irregularity came as a great surprise to me. What was happening?

Throughout this entire time, I do not believe that either of us have ever prayed and talked as seriously to God as we did about this exhaustion. We continued to believe that this was just a temporary situation, although it seemed to me like I was progressively getting worse. I could not understand it!

Another trip. I could hardly drag myself to the airport without wondering if I was going to make it. We got home on a Saturday afternoon and I headed straight for the bedroom, because I knew I was in another one of those "spells". A fleeting thought came—was it the pressure on the plane that gave me this?

I SLEPT FOR SIX STRAIGHT DAYS!

It seemed as if it took every ounce of everything I had in me to fight whatever was going on in my body to even come out of the fog I was in. It seemed as if I had to reach down into some deep, dark chasm to find any bit of intelligence. What I did find was not very much and certainly didn't last long.

For six straight days I did not have enough strength to put on clothes. I have never in my entire life felt so devoid of feeling, thinking or acting as I did during those six days. There were days when I wondered if I would ever come out of it. There were times when I wondered if I wanted to come out of it. Heaven would certainly be a lot better than this!

As I was struggling during this six-day war (and it was a real war), I decided to listen to some cassette tapes. It was impossible for me to even think about reading the Bible, but I knew the tapes would do something for me even while I was asleep. I put on a tape of Marilyn Hickey who has been my best friend for years. I love her and her wonderful, unique style of teaching. It always warms my heart.

I listened for about two sentences and said to myself, "What's the matter with her teaching on that tape? I can't stand her!"

I struggled to get the tape off of the cassette player. Laying it to one side, I fell off to sleep only to rouse out of my sleep enough to put on a Bob Tilton tape. He is another favorite of mine, but two sentences of him was all I could stand. I thought, "He is really irritating. I wonder how come I've always thought he was so outstanding!"

I tried John Osteen and the results were the same. Each one of them irritated me beyond belief!

I decided to play one of my own. I put on one of my best tapes that I recorded from the Living Bible and listened for one or two sentences and said, "I can't stand me either!"

I determined because the cassette tapes were so obnoxious that I would struggle to read the Bible. I tried to hold it in one hand and my eyes open with the other. I read about one or two sentences and the most unusual thought came floating by. I thought, "I've read that before. Who needs to read the Bible after you've read it once?"

The Bible slid off the bed and I slid back down into that bottomless pit and the world closed in behind me. The only thing I could say was, "God, God, God!"

The next moment of consciousness would find me saying, "Jesus, Jesus, Jesus!" I was incapable of praying for myself, but somehow my subconscious mind clung to the love of my life, God and Jesus!

During the time when these "spells" were at

their worst, we were writing our powerful book SUPERNATURAL HORIZONS. This is such an important end-generation book to lift the faith of the Body of Christ into where we are to be living in these last days before the return of Jesus.

Charles would stay at his typewriter until one or two o'clock every morning and be back writing again early the next morning. He was excited to see what was being written as God anointed him for this assignment and would bring a chapter or page to me to read. He was depending upon my reaction as a check on what he had just written and I would say, "Charles, I'll have to read it later, I am too tired to even think now." The last thing in the world I was interested in was trying to write a book!

Someway, God let me have recovery periods enough that we were finally able to complete the book with its full power and effect. How I praise Him for that!

I praise God for my wonderful husband. Throughout all of this, Charles probably suffered more than I did. There were great periods of time when I didn't even know I was suffering while his tender heart cried out to God to heal me, to touch me. Nothing seemed to do any good. His hurting was greater than mine.

One night when he came home from the office, I tried to get out of bed. I have never in my entire life felt so much like nothing as I did right then. I was totally incapable of any feeling or emotion and I said, "Honey, what I am about to say is not true and I know it. But I want you to know what I feel like inside."

I began to cry, "Honey, I'm sick!" I leaned against the wall as I tried to get to the bathroom. "I don't feel like I love you, I don't feel like I love me, and I don't even feel like I love God!" I screamed, "Charles, what is the matter with me?"

I believe in that moment the husband that I adore who knows how I love God, knew that I was really sick.

That's the last I remember until the six-day war was over. When I began to come out of the "spell," I realized that something was definitely wrong with me. I told Charles that as soon as I got over the "spell," I was going to the doctor and have every blood test made that can be made.

I didn't even feel that I could make a trip to the doctor's office in the condition I was in, but the time to go to a doctor is when you're sick, not when you're well.

Finally, I began feeling better. Charles took me to the doctor and we told him about the sleeping, the extreme exhaustion and the problem I had bringing my mind into a conscious state. I can understand a doctor wondering if a patient is a hypochondriac because at this point I once again looked hale and hearty. I didn't look as if I had been sick at all. It was difficult for me to tell him how miserable I had been because I couldn't even remember myself how horrible it had been.

He took a urinalysis which showed no problems whatsoever. Then he took several blood samples because I had fasted before coming to his office.

He took my blood pressure and it was even a little higher than the last time I had been there. I wondered again, "How can this be when God gave me a new heart on May 14, 1974?" I thought, "Why is my thyroid out of whack? Why is my blood pressure up when God healed me of both of those diseases?" The thyroid medication hadn't done me the least bit of good when I was having the "spell" but when I finally visited the doctor I looked like a real healthy specimen.

I returned two days after the blood tests had been taken.

I thought, "Oh, boy, now we'll know what's the matter. Charles will know how to pray for me to be healed!" That may sound like a strange statement for me to make, but I am thoroughly convinced that one of the greatest steps in receiving healing is to know what your problem is so you will know how to get healed.

Confident that I was going to discover the problem, I sailed into the doctor's office and he said, "I've got real good news for you. Your liver is perfect, this is perfect, this is perfect and this is perfect." He went right down the line saying, "Everything is perfect!"

Normally, that would be wonderful news and I praise God for all those good reports, but "perfect" wasn't exactly what I wanted to hear at that particular moment. I said, "That's not good news at all. I still don't know what's the matter with me. I'm not one of those women who enjoys being sick. I just want to know what my problem is."

None of this made sense to me at all because how could I have such perfect tests when I had just come through such a horrible session. I knew it was strictly of the devil, but I certainly wanted to know what the devil was trying to do to me.

He thought for a few moments and then said, "Frances, because of test number one and test number twenty-three, both of them being in the particular range that they are, you could have a 'hidden' disease." He continued, "I want you to fast again and come back tomorrow for a six-hour glucose tolerance test."

That was fine with me because I knew that no one in my family had ever had diabetes. I was willing to go through the test in order to eliminate one more disease, so I went home, fasted again and returned to his office bright and early the next morning.

The doctor came in after the initial testing and said, "Frances, you're starting at over the normal limit."

I didn't even realize that he was warning me about what was a suspicion in his mind but an impossibility in mine. I have confessed divine health for so long, it is impossible for my mind to conceive of some disease like diabetes, so I continued the test.

I had felt so good that day, I had taken along Sandy Brown's book, ISN'T THERE ANYBODY OUT THERE WHO CAN HELP ME? and between the routine blood and urine tests every half hour or hour, I edited her book. I was confident in the knowledge that God had His arm around me and that everything was going to be all right. After all, a person like me couldn't have diabetes!

Throughout the day, the nurse would ask, "How are you feeling?"

I would say, "Great, great, great" simply because that is a standard answer I always give when someones asks me how I feel. "Great, great, great..."

Before the test was totally completed, they called me into the doctor's office. My heart almost broke when I looked at him because I felt he must have had some bad news about a patient. I was right! The patient was me! He said, "Frances, I've got bad news for you. You're a *full-blown diabetic!*"

CHAPTER THREE

IT CAN'T BE HAPPENING TO ME!

I was stunned! This couldn't be happening to me. Instantly, all the people I have prayed for in healing lines who have lost their eyesight because of diabetes flashed into my mind. I thought about those who had lost their toes because of diabetes. Those who have had their legs amputated because of diabetes. What a horrible thought! This couldn't be happening to me! And yet, it was!

He continued, "I don't want you to ever taste sugar again. Don't eat white flour either." He continued on but I didn't hear anything else he said.

To me, it seemed as though he had just said, "Frances Hunter, I just signed your death certificate. Cause: Diabetes."

I praise God that I am full of the Word of God. I praise God for the more than 15,000 hours I have spent in His Word because what I said to him was not anything that I, as an individual and patient,

would have said to him. It was just something that
came right out of my inner being. I looked at him
with all the love in the world because he is a special
friend of ours, and said, "I rebuke that in the name
of Jesus. I do not receive it. I DO NOT RECEIVE
IT!"

I believe that statement is the very thing that
saved my life!

He said, "Frances, here's your chart." I took one
look and saw a miserable diabetic chart. The graph
showed my tests went to the top and blew it off,
then crashed to the bottom below the level of safety.

No wonder I had slept so long with my energy
level so low—I had gone repeatedly into DIABETIC
COMAS!

Hidden disease. The kind of diabetes you can
never diagnose through a urinalysis. It is discovered
only through a six-hour glucose tolerance test.

In almost a daze I listened as he prescribed the
medication and told me he would start me off with
small doses and increase them as I needed it.
Thoughts flashed through my mind, "Was that the
reason my big toes had felt so dead and without feeling for so long? Was that the reason the ulcer on my
leg did not heal until I went to the hospital and had
it debrided and then God healed it? Was that the
reason I had such an uncontrollable desire for
sweets?"

Charles had not gone with me to the doctor's office that day because neither of us suspected anything serious. We knew the test would take six hours
and Charles was busy at the office.

I got into the car to drive back to the office. I am glad Charles was not with me. If he had been there, I probably would have cried when the doctor gave me the bad news.

Our office is about an hour's drive from the doctor's office and I wanted to drive 100 miles an hour in order to get to Charles as fast as possible. Many people think that because I am a strong woman I am not dependent upon my husband, but I am just like a little homing pigeon. When something goes wrong with me, I want to flap my wings and fly to my husband as fast as I can. I could hardly wait for Charles to lay hands on me and pray.

When I'm sick, I don't want Oral Roberts to lay hands on me. I don't want Kenneth Hagin to lay hands on me. I don't want Kenneth Copeland to lay hands on me. I want CHARLES HUNTER to lay hands on me. *I know* what happens when my husband lays hands on me. I get healed! I remembered the new heart God inserted the night Charles took authority over my diseased heart! I wanted my husband!

As I drove along, I began to say, "Thank you, Lord; thank you, Lord; thank you, Lord that now I know what the problem is and when Charles lays hands on me, he'll know how to pray. He'll know what to do and then I know I'll get healed."

"Thank you, Lord; thank you, Lord, because at least I know what has been causing all this problem. I know I'm not senile. I know I'm not losing my mind."

All of a sudden, I was actually excited that I had

discovered I had diabetes. I set my car on cruise control. I was so anxious to get to Charles that I was afraid if I didn't, I might ignore the speed limit. As I drove along the highway back to our office, I began to think back to an anchor point in my life. We all have anchor points and at times they are one of the most valuable things you can have.

On February 4, 1978, we were at the Civic Center in Abilene, Texas. While we were ministering at the very beginning of the service, God stationed a huge warrior angel with us and spoke words which are burned into my heart. As I looked at this huge angel in complete astonishment and amazement because I had never before seen an angel, God said, "That's a special warrior angel I have sent to protect you and Charles from the fiery darts of the devil until Jesus Christ comes back again!"

In my car, I cried out from the very depths of my soul, "God, you promised me. YOU PROMISED ME that I would live to see the return of Jesus." Then, I added, "Devil, you can't have my life!"

I planned to break the news gently to Charles, but when I got to the office, I ran into Charles' office as fast as I could and blurted out, "The doctor said I'm a full-blown diabetic."

I had said it out loud and the impact really hit me! Charles quickly said, "Let's go home!"

We didn't mention my problem to anyone in the office. I felt a need to get home because it was four o'clock in the afternoon and I hadn't had anything to eat all day long. When we walked into the house, I turned on the TV to try to catch the weather forecast for the next day. We were leaving for another trip.

Our television set is one of those "instant" picture sets and there's no time to be warned by conversation. You just get the picture immediately and I could hardly believe what I saw on television.

A man pointed a long finger right at me and said, "Are YOU tired?"

Normally, I don't talk back to anyone on television, but I screamed right back at the television set, "YES!"

In the most dismal tone you could ever imagine, he somberly said, "You could have DIABETES." ("That's right," I thought, "the doctor just finished telling me that.") He continued, "THE THIRD BIGGEST KILLER IN THE WORLD IS DIABETES."

That was just exactly what I needed to hear! Heart disease is first, then cancer and third, diabetes. Then, he had to make the whole situation worse by saying, "And your DAUGHTER could have it, too!"

I said, "Charles, get Joan on the telephone real fast. She's got to have a glucose tolerance test made."

Charles turned to me and asked, "Honey, what exactly is diabetes?"

In the simplest way I knew how to describe it, I said, "It's when your pancreas does not produce enough insulin. The doctor has to prescribe insulin medication to make up for the lack of it in your body."

He said, "Is that all? Now, we know what to do."
We have seen and experienced many creative miracles—now it was another creative job for God! He
laid hands on the pancreatic area and said, "In the
name of Jesus, I command a new pancreas to come
into your body." Then, he thanked God that it had
been done.

That was all he said or did!

As I had left to go to the doctor's office early in
the morning, we had prayed and asked God to give
the doctor great wisdom to find whatever this "hidden" disease was so that we would know how to
pray. He had answered. In the only way we know
how to pray or heal the sick, God heard our cry.

I began to feel better as soon as I started on the
medication. I even called the doctor the day we left
town to report that the medication was having a
good effect. He said, "That's great, but if you start
feeling shaky or if you don't feel good again, just increase the medication slightly."

We were scheduled to speak at a Full Gospel
Businessmen's Fellowship Regional Convention in
Decatur, Illinois. After the first meeting, they invited us to come back to the hospitality room for
some refreshments. We walked in. It seemed to me
that there were thousands and thousands of fudge
squares, chocolate chip cookies, cakes and desserts
of all kinds!

Normally, these would have been real tempting
for me to plow into. However, I had begun to read
everything I could get my hands on concerning
sugar. The more I read, the more I became convinced

that sugar is a real killer! The doctor had told me sugar is just as addictive as cocaine and equally as bad for you. He said it is a cousin to cocaine. Then he graphically explained that it was the same principle as putting a little rat poison on your cereal every morning until you have eaten enough to kill you.

As a result of reading all this and hearing various people comment on the dangers of sugar, the temptation to eat anything with sugar in it completely vanished! I looked at this "sea" of cookies. All I could see was the skull and crossbones which appear on the side of every bottle of poison. I looked again, and the cookies disappeared and became a sea of nothing but skull and crossbones!

We had a wonderful weekend and I felt great. The doctor had given me a carefully regulated diet and I didn't stray from it one single bit or bite!

One of the very first things I noticed was that my mind seemed to have been cleared of the cobwebs which had sneaked in when I wasn't looking. Without even being aware of it, I began quoting scripture with no confusion or doubt. The ability to make decisions came back quickly and no longer did I have to "think" for an hour or so trying to decide if something should be printed in red or blue. The capability of my brain to make decisions seemed to be restored. My comprehension was once again normal, and I hadn't even been off of sugar for more than a week, and yet the results were absolutely astounding.

Once again my interest in the responsibilities I have in the ministry returned. No longer was I having to shove all of them off on Charles who was busy enough with his work. I began to think ahead. I began to plan ahead for the things we wanted to accomplish. Once again I had a desire to finish the book POSSESSING THE MIND OF CHRIST. I had started it more than three years before, but had never been able to complete it. Now the urgency and ability was there to see it finished! The devil had held my hand back long enough, because I had known all along that this was a book which God wanted in the hands of the Body of Christ.

I was faithful in taking the medication and continued to feel extremely well, and then one Friday morning I woke up with the knowledge that something was wrong. I crashed right down to rock bottom again. I felt miserable and couldn't understand it. Remembering the doctor had told me to increase the medication slightly if I had a bad day, I did just that, went to bed and promptly decided I felt worse.

We were scheduled to be on a radio-telethon program in the New Jersey area the next night, and here I was again, down at the bottom of the pit. I said to Charles, "Honey, I've got that same thing back all over again." He suggested that I stay in bed all day long because we knew I had to get up the next morning to fly half way across the country, and I certainly didn't feel up to it. I didn't even move out of bed that whole day long. I couldn't understand why I had responded so well to the medication and then suddenly it didn't seem to help at all.

Saturday morning rolled around, and even though I got out of bed, I said to Charles, "I don't think I can make it." God has never called me to do anything that He has not given me the power to do, so even though I was dragging, I thought that maybe if I could sleep for the entire three-and-a-half hour trip I might possibly feel better.

We drove to the airport, and as soon as we boarded the plane, I promptly fell asleep. Again it was with that horrible feeling of being drugged, a real "dead" sleep. Suddenly they made an announcement that we were going to have to land in Atlanta because of mechanical difficulties. We landed with no incident, but when I tried to get off of the plane, I was so exhausted I could hardly put one foot in front of the other.

I said to Charles, "Honey, I have never felt this miserable in my entire life."

I had to find a chair because I was so overcome with exhaustion I knew I would fall over if I didn't sit down. I found several chairs empty, so I sat down in one, but before a few seconds had passed, I had draped myself over another one, and then finally a third. I was desperate. I knew I could not make it to Philadelphia, and I knew that I could not make it back home. I felt that my consciousness was slipping away from me, and I didn't know what to do.

Should I let Charles go on without me, and should I try and get to a hotel in Atlanta and wait for him to come back for me? I didn't feel capable of taking care of myself and I almost panicked. I said, "Charles, I can't make it to Philadelphia and I can't make it back home!" The look on Charles face broke my heart because he felt so helpless. He had laid

hands on me on the plane, he had laid hands on me
as soon as I sat down. What else could he do?

Even though I was draped over three chairs in
the Atlanta airport, I started looking around on the
floor for a place to lie down that was clean enough. I
didn't care if it was out in the open where everyone
could see what I was doing, I just knew I was as sick
as I had ever been in my life.

I had my Bible in my hand when I disembarked
from the plane in Atlanta, and it was laying on my
lap. Suddenly it started to fall off. I had tried to read
it on the plane, but that was impossible, because I
could feel myself slipping right into another coma.

"God, where are you?"

I grabbed for the Bible, and all the things which
were inside started to fall on the floor. Charles
reached down to pick up the things that had fallen
out and I caught the Bible partially. With what
seemed to me to be superhuman strength, I lifted my
Bible which had fallen open onto my lap, and as I
did, my eyes fell on a scripture which I had under-
lined when I first got my New King James Version.
*Psalms 30:2 says, "O Lord my God, I cried out to
You, And You have healed me."*

I said, "But I don't feel like it."

I know there is healing in the Word of God, so as
I struggled between that thin line of a coma and ac-
tual reality, I said out loud, *"O Lord my God, I cried
out to You, And you have healed me."*   .

"But I don't feel like it."

*"O Lord my God, I cried out to You, And You
have healed me."*

I cried out, "But I don't feel like it."

"O Lord my God, I cried out to You, And You have healed me."

At least ten times I said that scripture out loud while Charles was watching me, and suddenly I remembered Gene Lilly who had been healed of diabetes in one of our services in Orlando, Florida. He took his insulin shot the next day and went into insulin shock and had to eat a dozen candy bars and drink a quart of orange juice to bring himself out of it.

I said, *"O Lord, my God, I cried out to You, And You have healed me,"* and I'm still on insulin and I'm putting myself into an insulin shock because you gave me a new pancreas that's working perfectly!"

I sat up and said, "Charles, get me some sugar! God healed me, God healed me! And what I've been doing is taking the medication and so I'm knocking .myself out in the other direction. Get me some candy quickly. Hurry, hurry!"

Charles took off like a shot out of a gun and returned quickly with a bar of candy. Although sugar is a real no-no, it is the thing that will bring you out of insulin shock, and how I praise God I remembered that.

I gulped the candy down, and within five minutes I began to improve and my energy began to return. We boarded the plane and they served a "gooey" dessert. Two huge cookies with about a half inch of marshmallow creme in the middle. I gobbled it down, and within fifteen minutes I felt like a million dollars.

We went on to Philadelphia where we were on radio until about two o'clock in the morning. I got up the next morning feeling great and looked at the insulin and decided to cut way back on it because something inside of me rebelled. I knew God had healed me, but I also remembered the advice we always give to everyone who is healed in our services: "Don't go off of your medication until your doctor tells you to."

We had three days of glory with double services each day, and I was never tired for a single moment during this time. I felt super great! We flew back home and I wasn't tired at all from the long flight, but went immediately into the office.

I fasted that night and the next morning, and called the doctor's office for an appointment. I told him that I really believed God had healed me completely of diabetes. I told him I felt that I had received a brand new pancreas when Charles laid hands on me.

This was hard even for a Spirit-filled doctor to accept because of his knowledge of medicine and how diabetes reacts. He took another blood test and when he came in to see me with the results, he was scratching his head and he said, "Frances Hunter, I don't know what I'm going to do with you. YOUR BLOOD IS ABSOLUTELY NORMAL! THROW AWAY ALL OF THAT MEDICATION." All of that medication. ALL of that medication.

I threw out the insulin. I tossed out the thyroid. God had won the battle again. My blood was completely free of that "hidden" disease, disinsulinism, which is a combination of both diabetes and hypo-glycemia.

Today, having just passed my sixty-eighth birthday, I can tell you that I feel better than I have in years. I look better than I have in years, and my weight is going down. At the time of this writing, within ninety days, I have already lost over twenty pounds with no effort on my part. I have completely eliminated the sugar and white flour from my meals.

My blood pressure has gone back to normal, having gone up because of the diabetes. The thyroid had been attacked because of the diabetes. Now it is also back to normal and everything is functioning perfectly. Glory to God! How we praise Him for His faithfulness.

You may wonder why I went back to the doctor after I knew I had been healed. The reason I did is because I believe with my heart and soul that God's healings will stand up under X-ray. They will stand up under blood tests, so you have no reason to fear when you go back to a doctor. God's healings will stand the closest scrutiny in the world!

God has given me a voice in the Body of Christ through books, crusades, television and radio ap-pearances. It is His desire that we prosper and be in health, even as our souls prosper. He does not want us sick. That's the work of the devil, but God has taken what the devil intended for a victory in his corner, and has turned it around for a victory for Himself, but also as a warning signal to the Body of Christ.

For the last few years I have heard a lot of

people say, "White sugar is harmful. It's as bad as cocaine." Those statements rolled right off of my back and I have answered back, "I've eaten it for years, and it hasn't hurt me."

I had to eat those words several months ago because I am thoroughly convinced that sugar is a killer.

We Christians have so spiritually fattened our minds in the last ten years with the Word, and we are so spiritually fat in that area, that we have ignored our bodies and what some of us have done to our bodies is unbelievable. We go to these great conventions and when the services are over, we run out and eat doughnuts and coffee, hot fudge sundaes, pecan pie or chocolate pie with whipped cream on top of it. I believe with my heart and soul that those fancy desserts and all that "good stuff" are absolutely nothing but a tool of the devil himself. If he can't get you one way, he'll try another. If he can't get you spiritually, he'll try to get you physically.

CHAPTER FOUR

I HATE SUGAR!

I haven't had one bite of sugar since that day in the Atlanta airport when I needed it to offset the insulin shock. I don't believe I will ever have a desire to eat anything sweet again because a flashing light immediately says, "POISON" and I see a skull and crossbones on every single dessert!

Twenty years ago God delivered me of cigarettes instantly! I had smoked for thirty-five years, and at the time of salvation, I was smoking five packages every single day. I went from five packs one day to nothing the next day!

Total abstinence from sugar is easy. Cutting down is like telling a delivered addict of alcohol or drugs to cut down. You don't cut down—you either totally stay away from your problem or you are back to heavy drinking or taking drugs. I believe sugar is exactly the same. I have had no "sugar" withdrawals and absolutely no temptation to take one sip, one trip, or one taste of sugar. Hallelujah!

The same principle applies to sin. It's much easier to clean up your life totally than it is to keep nibbling in sin because you're always a loser if you don't make a complete turnaround! Anyone who wants to keep having just an "occasional" piece of pie or cake is in real trouble because that little bit can drag you right back into your old habits. The only way to quit is QUIT!

What else has happened to me since I realized in the Atlanta airport that God healed me so dramatically and completely?

My mind is once again thinking clearly and quickly.

My ability to remember and retain has returned.

I am no longer tired.

I am loaded with energy.

My desire for Bible reading has returned in even greater measure than ever before in my entire life, and that's something, because I have always been a fanatic for the Word.

I'm listening avidly to cassette tapes again.

The desire to write books has returned.

I'm sleeping like a baby when I go to bed and I don't have the restless nights anymore.

I wake up in the morning earlier than ever before.

The retention of water which has been a problem all my life has disappeared. I just looked at a picture that was taken shortly before I discovered I had diabetes and I could hardly believe that my face was so puffed up. Even on the long trip home from Israel, I had no noticeable signs of swelling. After taking diuretics for fourteen years, I threw them away also because I don't have a water problem any more.

My weight is slowly but steadily decreasing and I am not always having to fight with dieting. I simply eat what I know is proper. I have discovered that bananas have a beautiful sweet taste. Cereal has a wonderful flavor without sugar. Strawberries are a wonderful dessert with nothing on them except possibly a little Equal which brings out the true sweetness of the strawberries.

I have discovered fresh vegetables are far more succulent without heavy salt and dressings. My taste buds, once deadened by sugar and salt are now capable of receiving satisfying signals from food the way God intended for it to be eaten.

Dr. Steve Gyland of Jacksonville, Florida, a friend of ours, called me to make a television commercial for him. I related to him the story of my diabetes and my subsequent healing. He sent me a book entitled LOW BLOOD SUGAR AND YOU, which has been a tremendous help in understanding the things that happened to me and relating them to other people so that they will not have to go through the horrible experience I did.

Dr. Gyland told me not only to totally eliminate the white sugar and flour, but said that chocolate and caffeine were real no-no's for a diabetic. He said caffeine has a bad effect on the pancreas.

I have always loved two cups of coffee in the

mornings, but it's an amazing thing when your life is at stake, you can give up ANYTHING! No longer do I have a desire for coffee. If I should take a soft drink, I drink a "no-cal, no-caffeine, no-taste" one. I finally decided it would be a lot better to drink plain water. As Charles always says, "God invented water and nobody has ever improved on it." When you decide to drink water, it certainly takes the indecision out of "What are we going to have to drink for dinner tonight?"

I believe it is time for the Body of Christ to wake up. We are trying to kill ourselves eating sugar and white flour. The only thing I have done to get more energy is to quit eating sugar and white flour. We're even quitting salt because they say the three white killers are flour, sugar and salt.

It is an interesting fact that we never think too much about our health until we have lost it. We take our good health for granted. I never really appreciated the tremendous strength God has given me throughout my life until I didn't have it any more. I am honest with you when I say I never went through such a terrible period in my entire life, and yet I am thanking God that He took a mess that the devil and I made and He has made a miracle out of it.

For dessert today, I eat a half a banana or a dish of strawberries and get all the sugar I need from fruit. With each meal, I eat a half of a banana or some other piece of fruit such as an apple or a pear, and my body is perfectly satisfied with the sugar it is getting.

I am not a doctor and don't pretend to have all

the answers, but hypoglycemia and diabetes basically fall into the same category because they are both the result of the pancreas malfunctioning.

Since I was so beautifully healed, I have shared my testimony across the nation. Each time I have, I asked to see the hands of those who are experiencing an energy lag or have extreme tiredness. I was amazed the first time because more than 75% of the people raised their hands. It has been the same with every audience since then. I ask the simple question, "How many of you eat more sugar than you know you should?" and the response is exactly the same.

I believe God is speaking to the Body of Christ and telling them to begin to be more attentive to what the Bible says in regard to foods. It even warns us against eating too much honey (because of the sugar content).

I talked to Dr. Gyland and told him of the tremendous number of people who stand because of a lack of energy. He said he believed that if every person in an audience would have a glucose tolerance test made, they would very likely discover that over 50 percent of the people who experience tiredness and loss of memory are borderline diabetics or borderline hypoglycemic individuals.

One of the reasons diabetes and hypoglycemia remain "hidden" diseases is because many doctors do not like to take six hours for such a test. It does tie up their nurses and lab technicians. Many individuals also do not like such tests which involve frequent blood and urine tests. However, "hidden" diseases such as these will not show up with just a urine test on a routine physical examination.

I praise God for my persistence and that I didn't give up but kept going back to the doctor until I found out what my problem was. I believe my persistence is why I am alive and well today.

Recently, I said to Charles, "Honey, do you realize that it is only because of the grace of God and the mercy of God that I am alive today? That alone was what kept me alive during those diabetic comas. God's hand was upon me even though I didn't realize it at the time.

God could have healed me at any time. Why did He choose to let me go through what I did? God is a loving God and He certainly doesn't want His children to suffer, so one day I decided to ask Him during one of my "talking to God" times.

I didn't mince any words with Him because He knows what I'm thinking anyway. There's no purpose in trying to fool God, so I said, "God, why didn't you heal me before you did? Why did you let me go through those terrible diabetic comas?"

His answer was beautiful. he said, "If I had healed you before you went to the doctor, you would never have known what I healed you of. And you would never have been able to tell the world about it!"

That was easy to understand, wasn't it? God wants this message brought to the Body of Christ. How could I have brought it if I had not discovered I had diabetes?

We have seen scores of people healed of diabetes and hypoglycemia since God healed me because

He has a whole warehouse of new pancreases available for those who want and need them.

We have also seen some very peculiar things happen when we ask God to put in a new pancreas. At one of our services in Oklahoma City, Charles laid hands on a man and when he got up off of the floor after being slain by the power of God, he clutched his trousers. He came running up to the stage and said, "I don't know what happened to me when you laid hands on me, but look at my pants!" He also showed how the sleeves on his shirt were loose where they had previously been tight. The next day he returned to the meetings to tell us that when he had gotten home that night, he weighed himself and had lost eighteen pounds! Glory!

Not to be outdone, I prayed for a lady in Florida who lost so much weight instantly during a diabetes healing that she completely lost her underpants! They fell right on the floor. She looked at me with great embarrassment and said, "What shall I do?"

I said, "Pick them up!"

A lady evangelist came to some meetings in Iowa and her suit was bulging when she tried to fasten the jacket. After the service when she was healed of diabetes, she could lap her jacket over more than four inches! God had done a supernatural work in her, too!

As you read this book, you may say what some have said to me already, "Why didn't you just stand on the Word? Why did you go to a doctor?" Then some have added, "Doesn't that show a lack of faith?"

I don't believe going to a doctor indicates any lack of faith. As I have explained before, we always go to God first, but if we don't get healed that way, then we take what God has also provided—help through the medical field.

I have as much faith as anyone I know. Charles and I have stepped out on spiritual water hundreds and even thousands of times and my faith never goes down because I visit a doctor occasionally! My faith is even stronger today because I know what I had, and I know what God healed! I give Him all the praise and glory!

A healing like mine always causes your mind to go off in a lot of other areas. I began to think about something else in my life that I have asked God to heal.

People have often asked me why I wear glasses and my standard response is, "So I can see!" Twenty years ago I had the lenses of my eyes removed. I am legally blind and wear both contacts and glasses with which I have miracle vision. The eye problem that I have is not really a problem because it has been corrected and my vision is much better than most individuals. I remember one time we asked Mel Tari if they still walked on the water in Indonesia. He said, "No."

Surprised, we asked, "Why?"

He said, "Because they built a bridge and we don't need to walk on the water anymore!"

I believe the same thing is true of my eyes. The bridge I have is glasses and contacts, but what would happen if glasses and contacts were outlawed? Would I get more serious with God about the eye problem?

I decided to discuss this situation with God. "Is it because I see with no problem with contacts and glasses that I have never gotten serious enough with You to receive new lenses in my eyes?"

Thinking back, I realize that with the diabetes I had really gotten serious with God. I got down to business when I discovered my problem. I have never cried out to God as much in my entire life as I did upon discovering diabetes in my own temple of God! Charles never cried out as much, even with my heart problem, as he did with the diabetes.

There is no healing for diabetes outside of God. I didn't like the things I knew about people who had diabetes—the bad eyes, the loss of toes, etc. I cried out to God with my entire body, mind and soul. And so did Charles. We knew it was either God or no healing.

God was faithful and how I love Him for it. There was no ignoring the sickness, there was no hoping that it might improve, it was just getting serious with God that made the difference. In a soft little voice God answered me back and said, "That's right, you were really serious about the diabetes, and you've never been serious about getting your eyes healed!"

CHAPTER FIVE

AN OUNCE OF PREVENTION

I want to help you so I am going to share with you the diet which the doctor gave me as just a little insight for you to see that it's not overly rigid, but certainly eliminates the things that can destroy your body. This is, of course, not the only diet so you may want to have your personal physician provide one for you.

II Corinthians 3:16,17 says, *"Do you not know that you are the temple of God and that the Spirit of God dwells in you? If anyone defiles the temple of God, God will destroy him. For the temple of God is holy, which temple you are."*

The diet has been planned to meet the specific nutritional needs of all individuals as you will see. You need to select the meal plan which provides you with the appropriate number of calories each day in a balanced nutritional intake for your particular weight. This specified caloric level is met by con-

suming the required number of servings in each
food group as indicated in your Daily Food Allowance.

The foods on the following list are divided into
six groups which are called Exchange Lists. Por-
tions of all foods within an Exchange List have ap-
proximately equal carbohydrate and caloric values.
By selecting different foods within each of the six
Exchange Lists you can add variety to your meals.
If, for example, you are to follow the 1600 Calorie
Diet, your lunch would be:

1	choice (or serving)	½	small banana
	from each of the	1 t.	butter
	fruit & bread	1	biscuit or slice
	Exchange Lists		of whole wheat
			bread
1	serving from the		Any amount of
	veg. "A" List		raw cucumbers.
			Vinegar/spices
			as desired.
2	servings/Meat	1 oz	chicken
	Exchange List	1	egg, or
		2 oz	meat (no fat)

Water, caffeine-free coffee or herb tea as desired.

In between meals it is recommended that you
enjoy an eight-ounce protein drink. I mix mine in
my blender with a couple of cubes of ice, a package
of Equal and whip it to the frothy stage. It's delicious! This is particularly good for the person with
hypoglycemia who needs that in-between-meal
snack.

It is very important that you eat the amounts

and kinds of food indicated in the Daily Food Allowance program. The nutritive value of your meals and nourishments has been arranged by specialists to provide you with balanced nutrition throughout the day. We should always be careful not to eliminate any of the foods indicated in the Daily Food Allowance. We've learned to be careful of the portions, too.

DAILY FOOD ALLOWANCE

(Select from Exchange Lists on the next pages)

	Number of Servings for:				
	1000 Cal.	1400 Cal.	1600 Cal.	1800 Cal.	2000 Cal.
BREAKFAST					
Fruit	1	1	1	1	1
Meat	1	1	1	1	1
Bread	½	1	2	1	2
Fat	-	1	2	2	2
Coffee or tea (as desired)					
MID-MORNING					
Protein drink	-	-	-	1	1
LUNCH					
Meat	2	2	2	2	3
Vegetable list A	1	1	1	1	1
Bread	-	1	1	1	1
Fat	-	1	1	1	1
Fruit	1	1	1	1	1
Coffee or tea (as desired)					
MID-AFTERNOON					
Protein drink	1	1	1	1	1

DINNER					
Meat	3	3	3	3	4
Vegetable list A	1	1	1	1	1
Vegetable list B	1	1	1	1	1
Bread	-	1	1	1	1
Fat	-	1	1	1	1
Fruit	1	1	1	1	1

EVENING					
Protein drink	1	1	1	1	1

FOOD GROUPS
VEGETABLE "A" EXCHANGE

Amount Per Serving   raw-any amount
cooked-1 cup

Asparagus	Lettuce
Broccoli	Mushrooms
Brussels sprouts	Okra
Cabbage	Peppers
Cauliflower	Radishes
Celery	Sauerkraut
Cucumbers	Spinach
Eggplant	Summer squash
Green beans	Tomatoes*
Greens	Wax beans

*Limit to one tomato or ½ cup tomato juice per serving.

VEGETABLE "B" EXCHANGE

Amount Per Serving: Raw/cooked-½cup

Beets	Pumpkin
Carrots	Rutabagas
Onions	Turnips
Peas	Winter Squash

BREAD EXCHANGE

	Amount Per Serving
Bread	1 slice
Biscuit	1
Crackers, saltine	5
Graham	2
Round thin	6
Muffin, plain	1
Cereal, cooked	½ cup
Dry	¾ cup
(not presweetened)	¾ cup
Potatoes, white	½ cup
Potatoes, sweet	¼ cup
Rice (cooked)	½ cup
Spaghetti noodles (cooked)	½ cup
Macaroni (cooked)	½ cup
Egg noodles (cooked)	½ cup
Corn	⅓ cup
Lima beans	½ cup
Baked beans	¼ cup
Angelfood cake	1 in. slice
Sponge cake	1½ in. cube
Vanilla wafers	5

MEAT EXCHANGE

Baked, boiled or broiled:

	Amount Per Serving
Meat, poultry, fish (lean)	1 ounce
Luncheon meats	1 ounce
Oysters, clams, shrimp	5 small
Tuna, salmon (water pack)	¼ cup
Egg	1
Cheese	1 ounce

Cottage cheese   ¼ cup
Peanut butter   1 Tbsp.

FRUIT EXCHANGE
Fresh, frozen or canned without sugar:

	Amount Per Serving
Apple (2 in. diam.)	1 small
Apple juice	⅓ cup
Applesauce	½ cup
Apricots	2 medium
Apricot nectar	⅓ cup
Banana	½ small
Blackberries	1 cup
Blueberries	⅔ cup
Cantaloupe (6 in. diam.)	¼
Cherries	10 large
Dates	2
Grapefruit	½ small
Grapefruit juice	½ cup
Grape juice	¼ cup
Grapes	12 large
Honeydew melon	1 in. slice
Nectarine	1 medium
Orange	1 sm.
Orange juice	½ cup
Peach	1 medium
Pear	1 small
Pineapple	½ cup
Pineapple juice	⅓ cup
Plums	2 medium
Prunes, dried	2 medium
Prune juice	¼ cup
Raisins	2 Tbsp.
Raspberries	1 cup
Strawberries	1 cup

Tangerine	1 large
Watermelon	1 cup

FAT EXCHANGE

	Amount Per Serving
Butter or margarine	1 tsp.
Heavy cream	1 Tbsp.
Light cream	2 Tbsp.
Mayonnaise or oil	1 tsp.
French dressing	1 Tbsp.
Cream cheese	1 Tbsp.
Bacon	1 slice
Olives	5
Nuts	6 small
Avocado	½ in. slice

ALLOWED AS DESIRED
Foods
Artificially sweetened decaffeinated coffee or caffeine free beverages with less than 10 calories/can, fat free broth or bouillion rhubarb or cranberries (no sugar aded), sour or dill pickles, unflavored gelatin.
Seasonings
Herbs, spices, salt, mustard, lemon, flavor extracts, calorie-free sugar substitutes, vinegar.

MEASURING FOOD:
Portion sizes must be accurate; weigh or measure when necessary. For this, all you will need is a standard 8 ounce measuring cup and measuring spoons. All measurements are level. Cooked foods are measured after cooking. The use of a small scale to determine portion sizes is helpful until you are familiar with the appearance of the correct serving size.

FOOD PREPARATION:

Meats may be baked, boiled or broiled. Your foods may be prepared with the family meals, but be sure your portion is removed before any extra fat or flour is added. We think it's a good idea if the whole family eats wisely, so let them eat with you! Fried foods should be eaten only if an allowed fat choice is used for frying; combination dishes such as stews and casseroles may be eaten if permitted ingredients are used in the amounts specified in your Daily Food Allowance.

AVOID THESE FOODS:

Sugar, candy, honey, jam, jelly, preserves, marmalade, syrup, pies, cakes and cookies, pastries, condensed milk, sweetened carbonated beverages, chewing gums containing sugar, fried, scalloped and creamed foods, and snack items such as pretzels, popcorn and potato chips.

- - - -

Have a family conference and decide right now that you are going to live in divine health, and that the first step is to get rid of sugar and to retrain the appetite of your family. You do your part and God will do His part!

Charles and I take Cambridge or some other protein drink on the road with us. We have a little "minimikser" which operates on batteries and works beautifully for anyone who works in an office or, like us, is on the road. We add a couple of ice cubes to cool it down, a package of Equal or other appropriate sugar substitute and it works fine!

In my heart there keeps ringing a warning bell

to the Body of Christ. Jesus said, *"See, you have been made well. Sin no more, lest a worse thing come upon you."* (John 5:14). To me, He said, "Frances, go and eat sugar no more, lest a worse thing come upon you!"

I am more aware of the diabetics and hypoglycemics than ever before as we lay hands on them night after night. My heart cries for the individuals whose bodies are covered with sores which won't heal, whose eyesight is failing, and whose energy is gone. Each time I lay hands on one and believe for a new pancreas for them, I thank God that He saw fit to give me a new one which is functioning beautifully!

But my heart probably cries more for another reason than when I lay hands on them for a new pancreas. After all the warnings I give them at the meetings about the dangers of sugar, we see them eating in restaurants after the meetings and gorging themselves on pies, cakes and coffee, totally disregarding the warning flags God has put out.

We all love Christian fellowship after meetings but we need to begin to exercise caution. If you want to drink coffee because you like something warm, drink brewed decaffeinated coffee. Most restaurants have both types today. You can tell it by the orange top on the coffee pot. If they don't have it, drink hot water. You have no idea how good hot water can be with a meal. And if you haven't tried it yet, don't complain about it because it will surprise you.

CHAPTER SIX

GOD'S GOOD FOOD

A very interesting article written by J.A. Dennis of Kerrville, Texas was given to me recently. He is now 85 and his wife is 80. I felt it was so good it should be shared with the entire Body of Christ, so I am quoting it here with their permission.

Frances

GOD'S GOOD FOOD

"If you diligently heed the voice of the Lord your God and do what is right in His sight, give ear to His commandments and keep all His statutes, I will put none of the diseases on you which I have brought on the Egyptians. For I am the Lord who heals you"(Exodus 15:26).

The last few years I have become increasingly
convinced that what we eat has a tremendous bearing on our state of health. The factors that are necessary in our staying well, in my opinion, in the order
of their importance, are:

1. Our faith in God's promises to heal us and
keep us free from sickness.

> *"No evil shall befall you, Nor shall any*
> *plague come near your dwelling;"*
> (Psalm 91:10)
> *"For I am the Lord who heals you"*
> (Exodus 15:26).
> *"Beloved, I wish above all things that*
> *thou mayest prosper and be in health,*
> *even as thy soul prospereth"* (III John 2
> KJV).
> *"He Himself took our infirmities And*
> *bore our sicknesses"* (Matthew 8:17).
> *"Who Himself bore our sins in His own*
> *body on the tree, that we, having died*
> *to sins, might live for righteousness—*
> *by whose stripes you were healed"* (I
> Peter 2:24).

2. The kind and amount of food and drink we
take into our bodies.

> *"You shall not eat any detestable*
> *thing"* (Deuteronomy 14:3).
> *"So you shall serve the Lord your God,*
> *and He will bless your bread and your*
> *water. And I will take sickness away*
> *from the midst of you"* (Exodus 23:25).

3. The exercise and fresh air we give our bodies.
*"My Father has been working until now,
and I have been working"* (John 5:17).
*"I must walk today, and tomorrow, and the
day following"* (Luke 13:33 KJV).
*"For even when we were with you, we com-
manded you this: If anyone will not work,
neither shall he eat"* (II Thessalonians
3:10).
4. The rest that we take in peaceful sleep.
*"I will both lie down in peace, and sleep;
For You alone, O Lord, make me dwell in
safety"* (Psalm 4:8).
*"It is vain for you to rise up early, To sit up
late, To eat the bread of sorrows* (to worry);
For so He gives His beloved sleep" (Psalm
127:2).
5. The peace of mind which comes when we are
at peace with ourselves, with God, and with man.
*"Come to Me, all you who labor and are
heavy laden, and I will give you rest. Take
My yoke upon you and learn from Me, for I
am gentle and lowly in heart, and you will
find rest for your souls. For My yoke is easy
and My burden is light"* (Matthew 11:28-
30).
*"Be anxious for nothing, but in everything
by prayer and supplication, with
thanksgiving, let your requests be made
known to God; and the peace of God, which
surpasses all understanding, will guard
your hearts and minds through Jesus*

Christ" (Philippians 4:6-7).

I have written numerous articles on the first item and firmly believe that it is God's will for His children to be well, just as human parents will do everything possible to keep their children from being sick, and that it is possible for Christians, by faith in His promises and His *"taking our infirmities and bearing our sicknesses,"* to stay well and strong, that they might serve the Lord effectively, and give and live a victorious testimony before others.

"For the Lord is our Judge, The Lord is our Lawgiver, The Lord is our King; He will save us;...And the inhabitant will not say, 'I am sick'; The people who dwell in it will be forgiven their iniquity" (Isaiah 33:22,24).

PROPER EATING

Many, many people today are food conscious. Diets are on every tongue, vitamins in every cupboard, "food faddists" on every corner. One "authority" would have you eat no meat; the next prescribes a "high protein" diet with plenty of meat; another forbids milk, another eggs, another salt, another cheese, etc., etc.

Everyone that has a theory, writes a book on it, and thousands scramble to buy it, if it promises them health with little effort and no sacrifice.

One diet might benefit one person and not agree with another. Our dear Brother Rufus Moseley, though frail and sickly as a youth, lived to be 83 on a diet made up principally of fruit and raw peanuts, but when I tried it, all I got was a "good" stomach ache.

After trying one theory, then another, I finally decided that God knew more than any man about eating as well as any other question. Had He not made these marvelous bodies? And should He not know what is the proper food for them? And had He not told us what to eat and what not to eat?

A search of God's Word showed me that God was interested in what His children ate, and that He had given some specific instructions regarding our diet. And I announced to my wife and others that as much as I loved and revered Brother Rufus, "I was going to follow God and Moses, rather than Moseley."

Some folks ridicule anyone who dares to quote Moses and God's separation of clean and unclean meats, shouting that "we are no longer under the Law!" Of course we are not, but, if Christians, we are still under God and His wisdom, and He and His wisdom are just the same today as in Moses' day, and our bodies are the same, also. What was good for man to eat in the Promised Land of Canaan, is still good for man today; and what was harmful for man then, is still harmful today.

Yes, "the proof of the pudding is in the eating," and the proof of God's loving wisdom is found in the fact that when man obeyed God's laws, He kept them well; while today, as we flaunt His advice and His Word our hospitals are overflowing, every doctor's waiting room is crowded, millions suffer pain and affliction, disease is everywhere. Scientists and health organizations spend years and millions of dollars trying to find the cause of so much sickness, but I fear they do not look in the right place—in God's Word, and to man's disobedience to Him.

God has put His stamp of divine approval on many foods. Some He has rejected or forbidden. Many today look for the seal of approval from Good Housekeeping or some other institute, or trade mark or brand name, or some doctor's prescription, but never think to ask if it has been stamped with God's approval.

When I began to seriously "search the Scriptures," to find out what God's Word said about what we should eat, I was amazed and delighted to learn that He had said so much, had approved so many items that modern "nutritionists" had ruled out as harmful.

PORK FORBIDDEN

The first item on my diet that had to pass God's scrutiny was pork. Like many others, I thought breakfast without "bacon and eggs" just wasn't breakfast. But God's Word said it was an "abomination" or "detestable thing", so it had to go.

"Also the swine is unclean for you, because it has cloven hooves, yet does not chew the cud; you shall not eat their flesh or touch their dead carcasses" (Deuteronomy 14:8).

"For behold, the Lord will come with fire
And with His chariots, like a whirlwind,
To render His anger with fury,
And His rebuke with flames of fire.
For by fire and by His sword
The Lord will judge all flesh;

And the slain of the Lord shall by many.
'Those who sanctify themselves
                    and purify themselves,
To go to the gardens
After an idol in the midst,
Eating swine's flesh and
the abomination and the mouse,
Shall be consumed together,' says the Lord"
                    (Isaiah 66:15-17).

"Behind one tree in the midst!" As God tested Adam and Eve and their faith, and obedience to His wisdom, by forbidding them to eat the fruit of the tree that grew in the midst of the Garden of Eden, so God tested the Israelites' faith and obedience (and ours) by forbidding the eating of swine's flesh.

And just as Eve reasoned with herself (with Satan's help) that the fruit was nice looking and good tasting and that God didn't really mean disobedience meant death, so have men to our day reasoned that anything that tasted as good as sweet, juicy pork was surely meant to be eaten, and surely eating it would not bring disease or death, even though in both cases, God has spoken otherwise.

Americans today eat millions of pounds of pork, and millions and millions are sick, never stopping to consider what God has said about what they should eat.

God put his stamp of approval on the eating of beef, when properly bled, and some other meats, PROVIDED the FAT and the BLOOD WERE NOT EATEN.

"These are the animals which you may

eat: the ox, the sheep, the goat, the deer, the gazelle, the roe deer, the wild goat, the mountain goat, the antelope, and the mountain sheep. And you may eat every animal with cloven hooves, having the hoof split into two parts, and that chews the cud, among the animals...

"These you may eat of all that are in the waters: you may eat all that have fins and scales. And whatever does not have fins and scales you shall not eat; it is unclean for you" (Deuteronomy 14:4-6,9).

"'This shall be a perpetual statute throughout your generations in all your dwellings: you shall eat neither fat nor blood'" (Leviticus 3:17).

Eve's sin in the Garden was to try to reason out a plausible excuse for disobeying God's command, rather than take it from One who had all wisdom and power.

So it is today among the pork eaters. They say, "We are not under the Law; Jesus made all meats clean; Paul said, 'Every creature of God is good, and nothing to be refused, if it be received with thanksgiving'; When Peter saw the vision of the unclean animals let down in the sheet and heard God say, *'What God has cleansed you must not call common'* (Acts 10:15) that made pork and all other meat clean." So does man reason, seeking to get around God's Word.

They who would quote Paul's statement in I Timothy 4:4, fail to quote the next verse, *"For it is sanctified by the word of God and prayer."* Pork has nowhere in God's Word been sanctified for food, but rather called detestable or an abomination.

Those who rely on Peter's vision as an excuse, overlook the fact that Peter was puzzled by the vision and did not know what it meant until he received the call from the Gentile Cornelius, and then he explained what it meant: *"But God has shown me that I should not call any man common or unclean"* (Acts 10:28).

Brother Rufus Moseley's stock answer to those who came asking, "Brother Moseley, don't you think I can eat pork and still go to Heaven?" was: "Oh, yes, and you will probably go much quicker, if you eat pork!"

But if one would agree that God knows best and wish to convince others that they could enjoy better health by observing God's commandments, there are many facts which show the wisdom and love of God in forbidding His children to eat pork!

Most authorities would admit that pork is very fat and very acid. Also, pork is known to contain parasites that infest our bodies, unless killed in the cooking. It is a rich source of cholesterol, now revealed as enemy of the heart and arteries. It causes scurvy when eaten in quantities without greens or green vegetables. Hogs are scavengers, and love to feed on dead cattle and horses.

If you examine the list of clean and unclean beasts in God's work, you see that all clean or "ap-

proved" meat comes from grass eating animals—
none from scavengers or from meat-eating animals.

I leave this matter of clean and unclean meats
for you to pursue in God's Word, for I know you love
Him and respect His Wisdom.

GOD'S APPROVED LIST

As to fish, the clean and unclean are listed.
Jesus, after His resurrection, ate fish and hon-
eycomb, and cooked a fish breakfast for his tired
and discouraged fisher-disciples. (John 21:9-13).

Jesus, the night before His crucifixion, ate the
Passover with the twelve in the upper room. (Luke
22:15).

Jesus called an egg a "good gift," saying the
same of bread and fish. (Luke 11:12-13).

The land of Canaan was described as a land
"flowing with milk and honey" thus putting God's
stamp of approval on these items.

Other foods on God's approved list include:

GRAPES: *"When you come into your neighbor's
vineyard, you may eat your fill of grapes at your
pleasure..."* (Deuteronomy 23:24).

FIGS: *"Then they came to the Valley of Eshcol, and
there cut down a branch with one cluster of grapes;
they carried it between two of them on a pole. They
also brought some of the pomegranates and figs"*
(Numbers 13:23).

*"Now the next day, when they had come out
from Bethany, He was hungry. And seeing from afar*

*a fig tree having leaves, He went to see if perhaps He would find something on it..."*Mark 11:12,13).

APPLES: *"The vine has dried up, And the fig tree has withered; The pomegranate tree, The palm tree also, And the apple tree—All of the trees of the field are withered; Surely joy withered away from the sons of men"* (Joel 1:12).

POMEGRANATES: *"...They also brought some of the pomegranates and figs"* (Numbers 13:23).

PALM DATES: *"And you shall take for yourselves on the first day the fruit of beautiful trees, branches of palm trees, the boughs of leafy trees, and willows of the brook; and you shall rejoice before the Lord your God for seven days"* (Leviticus 23:40).

ALL FRUITS: *"And God said, See I have given you every herb that yields seed which is on the face of all the earth, and every tree whose fruit yields seed; to you it shall be for food"* (Genesis 1:29).

HERBS: Same as ALL FRUITS.

OLIVES: *"A land of wheat and barley, of vines and fig trees and pomegranates, a land of olive oil and honey"* (Deuteronomy 8:8).

OLIVE OIL: *" And if you bring as an offering a grain offering baked in the oven, it shall be unleavened cakes of fine flour mixed with oil, or unleavened*

*wafers anointed with oil. But if your offering is a
grain offering baked in a pan, it shall be of fine flour,
unleavened, mixed with oil. You shall break it in
pieces and pour oil on it; it is a grain offering. And if
your offering is a grain offering baked in a covered
pan, it shall be made of fine flour with oil"* (Leviticus
2:4-7).

WHEAT: *"He would have fed them also with the
finest of wheat; And with honey from the rock I
would have satisfied you"* (Psalm 81:16).

BREAD: *"And He took bread, gave thanks and
broke it, and gave it to them, saying..."* (Luke 22:19).

CORN: *"And Boaz said unto her, At mealtime come
thou hither, and eat of the bread, and dip thy morsel
in the vinegar...And he reached her parched corn,
and she did eat, and was sufficed, and left"* (Ruth
2:14 KJV).
    *"And Jesse said unto David his son, Take now
for thy brethren an ephah of this parched corn, and
these ten loaves, and run to the camp to thy brethren;"* (I Samuel 17:17 KJV).

ROASTING EARS: *"And there came a man from
Baal-shalisha, and brought the man of God bread of
the firstfruits, twenty loaves of barley, and full ears
of corn in the husk thereof. And he said, Give unto
the people, that they may eat."* II Kings 4:42 KJV).
    *"And if thou offer a meat offering of thy
firstfruits unto the Lord, thou shalt offer for the
meat offering of thy firstfruits green ears of corn*

dried by the fire, even corn beaten out of full ears" (Leviticus 2:14 KJV).

BARLEY: "*So she stayed close by the young women of Boaz, to glean until the end of barley harvest and wheat harvest; and she dwelt with her mother-in-law*" (Ruth 2:23).

SALT: "*And every offering of your grain offering you shall season with salt; you shall not allow the salt of the covenant of your God to be lacking from your grain offering. With all your offerings you shall offer salt*" (Leviticus 2:13).

"*Salt is good, but if the salt loses its flavor, how will you season it? Have salt in yourselves, and have peace with one another*" (Mark 9:50).

HONEY: "*And with honey from the rock I would have satisfied you*" (Psalm 81:16).

POTTAGE (STEW): "*And Elisha returned to Gilgal, and there was a famine in the land. Now the sons of the prophets were sitting before him; and he said to his servant, Put on the large pot, and boil stew for the sons of the prophets*" (II Kings 4:38).

MILK: "*So it shall be, from the abundance of milk they give, that he will eat curds; For curds and honey everyone will eat who is left in the land*" (Isaiah 7:22).

BUTTER: *"And it shall come to pass in that day, that a man shall nourish a young cow, and two sheep; And it shall come to pass, for the abundance of milk that they shall give he shall eat butter; for butter and honey shall everyone eat that is left in the land"* (Isaiah 7:21,22 KJV).

CHEESE: *"And carry these ten cheese to the captain of their thousand, and see how your brothers fare, and bring back news of them"* (I Samuel 17:18).

GOAT'S MILK: *"You shall have enough goats' milk for your food, For the food of your household, And the nourishment of your maidservants"* (Proverbs 27:27).

LOCUSTS, GRASSHOPPERS: *"These you may eat: the locust after its kind, the destroying locust after its kind, the cricket after its kind, and the grasshopper after its kind. But all other flying insects which have four feet shall be an abomination to you"* (Leviticus 11:22,23).

(Special note from Frances Hunter: Praise God that He didn't say you SHALL eat. He just said you MAY eat! Charles says, "We are repulsed at the thought of eating crickets, grasshoppers, and locusts which God sanctioned, but we devour pork which God said was an abomination. Isn't that just like the devil to reverse God's menu?")

ALMONDS: *"And their father Israel said to them,*

'If it must be so, then do this: Take some of the best fruits of the land in your vessels and carry down a present for the man—a little balm and a little honey, spices and myrrh, pistachio nuts and almonds" (Genesis 43:11).

NUTS: Same as above—Old King James says "nuts".

BEEF: "And you may eat every animal with cloven hooves, having the hoof split into two parts, and that chews the cud, among the animals" (Deuteronomy 14:6)

MUTTON: "These are the animals which you may eat: the ox, the sheep, the goat" (Deuteronomy 14:4).

GOAT MEAT: Same as above.

FISH: "Then, as soon as they had come to land, they saw a fire of coals there, and fish laid on it, and bread. Jesus said to them, 'Bring some of the fish which you have just caught.' Simon Peter went up and dragged the net to land, full of large fish, one hundred and fifty-three; and although there were so many, the net was not broken. Jesus said to them, 'Come and eat breakfast'" (John 21:9-12).

EGGS: "Or if he asks for an egg, will he offer him a scorpion?" (Luke 11:12).

VENISON: "These are the animals you shall

eat...the deer, the gazelle, the roe deer, the wild goat, the mountain goat, the antelope, and the mountain sheep" (Deuteronomy 14:4,5).

Strong drink is forbidden to God's children and no sensible person today could question God's wisdom here, when we see the wrecks, both of cars and men, that result from drink. America is fast becoming a nation of drunkards and in danger of going the way of all drunken nations before her.

(Frances: Since we are the temple of God and are priests in His kingdom, read Leviticus 10:9: *"Do not drink wine or intoxicating drink, you, nor your sons with you, when you go into the tabernacle of meeting, lest you die. It shall be a statute forever throughout your generation.")*

The crux of the whole question is whether we will believe that God is all-good and all-wise and all-loving, and knows much better what is good for us than we do ourselves; or whether we think, as did Eve, that His ideas are "old fogey" and His commandments can be broken with impunity.

The safe rule in our eating is to make everything we eat, if not classified in God's Word and approved by Him, pass this test:

"Therefore, whether you eat or drink, or whatever you do, do all to the glory of God" (I Corinthians 10:31).

Can you glorify God by eating something because we "like it," when He has forbidden it?

Can you glorify God by drinking intoxicating

beverages when He has forbidden it?

Can you glorify God by smoking, when tobacco is known to be harmful and often dangerous to heart and lungs?

Can you glorify God by eating many of the rich, spicy, sticky "messes" that many people consume?

Paul warned of some whose God was their belly, and we have many such today. (Philippians 3:19).

God has been progressively, over the years, teaching me how and what to eat. A number of years ago we felt impressed to stop eating pork, and I found myself less susceptible to colds, as well as inwardly blessed, as we always are when we obey God.

For many years I had suffered hours and hours of pain in my stomach, brought on by ignorance of eating, as well as worry, nervousness, and emotional upset, many things I "couldn't eat". They would upset my stomach and cause nausea and pain. About five times I was dangerously sick with food poisoning from old grease, tainted meat, swollen canned corn, salad dressing, and spoiled milk. On top of that, I suffered from chronic indigestion, colds, frequent attacks of influenza, sinus trouble, hay fever.

HEALED

Then the Lord gave me the grace to stand on His promise in Exodus 23:35: *"So you shall serve the Lord your God, and He will bless your bread and your water. And I will take sickness away from the*

MIDST of you," for that's where I was sick, right in my "middle."

And praise the Lord for His goodness and power. He has been my only Physician for some 38 years, and the Bible and His grace my daily medicine. When I begin to feel badly, I take a "Gospil," rebuke the devil, and thank God for keeping me well. And, to His glory, I can say that He has not suffered me to miss a day's activities because of sickness in the past 38 years. There hasn't been a day when I was not able to get up and "put my shoes on" and go about His business.

Years ago when I was suffering with my stomach, a dear old lady told me that, if I asked God to, He would tell me what to eat that was good for me. I never forgot that, though it was a long time afterwards before I did much about it. Years later I came upon that promise:

"Who satisfies your mouth with good things, So that your youth is renewed like the eagle's" (Psalms 103:5).

"Good things!" I began to put the taste test to some things (not a perverted taste for harmful things). I found good beef, steak or roast, if properly cooked, tasted "good" and made me feel "good". I had never found any vegetarian diet that had the same effect. I found the fruit and nuts and raw vegetables such as lettuce, carrots, celery, tasted "good" and were "good" for me. Milk was "good," so was butter (real butter-no margarine for me), and eggs and beans, and whole wheat cereal, whole wheat bread, raw apples, peaches, grapes, pears;

sun-dried dates, raisins, prunes; baked potatoes, rightly cooked beets, carrots, turnips, corn, peas, and asparagus; whole oranges, grapefruit, pecans, almonds.

I learned from reading and experience that in most cases food in its natural state—the way God made it—was better, and better for you than when "processed" and "messed up" by man, notwithstanding all the high powered advertising over radio, newspaper, etc., of packaged foods.

This past year we learned another step: to eat simpler meals, not so many different foods at one meal, and to eat starches together, such as cereal and bread with milk; and proteins and acid food together, as meats with apples and oranges, but not with bread or milk.

I know there are a lot of fads in these respects and we are not dogmatic in our advice or our eating. When we eat out, or with friends, we eat "what is set before us" as Jesus told His disciples, but passing up the pork and the rich desserts.

After a meal with some of the rich, greasy food and sticky sweet desserts that some serve, I can prove in my own body the wisdom of God's approved list.

Here's a sample of a day's menu at our house:

BREAKFAST: Orange juice or half an apple; bowl of cooked cereal with half and half (steel cut whole wheat, flax, soy, wheat germ); buttered toast, of bread made from stone ground whole wheat flour (my wife makes our own bread); glass of milk; a few sun-dried dates or raisins and three or four raw almonds.

NOON MEAL: Beef roast; pinto beans; baked sweet potato; raw carrots, celery, lettuce; or cooked beets or cabbage; an apple or raw grapes; almonds.

SUPPER: Half an orange, beef steak; baked Irish potato; raw celery, lettuce, grapes or dried dates, almonds or pecans.

The proof with us, IS in the "pudding," for we feel younger, happier and healthier than for many years, though I am 85 and my wife 80, but many can hardly believe it.

I walk from one to five miles a day and can work all day at writing, keeping books, or typing, and then write letters "half the nite," without feeling worn out. And I thank the Lord that He has satisfied our mouths with good things so that our youth IS renewed like the eagle's.

EXERCISE

Along with food, must come proper exercise. America is becoming a "sit-down" nation. The average person would hesitate to go more than a block or two unless he rode in a car. We sit at a desk, we sit at entertainments, we sit in church, we sit and sit and sit. And our muscles grow soft and flabby, our resistance low, and every chill wind wreaks havoc upon us.

We need every day to work or walk or play in God's outdoor sunshine and fresh air. We breathe gasoline and gas stove fumes, cigarette and cigar smoke, all day and much of the night, and wonder why our lungs are weak. By failing to exercise until our lungs must pump in gallons and gallons of fresh air to carry off toxic poisons, we suffer weak hearts, hardened arteries, constipation, weak lungs, poor digestion, etc., etc.

SLEEP

We need restful natural sleep, and plenty of it. Sometimes after a very exhausting day, when I am too tired to write or read or even to think, I spend nine or ten hours in a good bed, and get up feeling fine again. Millions today go to bed with sleeping pills, many because they are not at peace with God or their fellows or themselves. But God has promised His children sleep. And I thank Him for it every night when I go to bed, and every morning when I wake up. (Psalm 4:8; Psalm 127:2).

We have no fears to keep us awake, even though our doors are not locked at night. We have no worries over money or health, because we have committed ourselves and our keeping over to Him who "is able to keep that which is committed unto Him."

God has invited us to enter into His rest, and cease from our own fearful, fitful efforts to save the world or ourselves.

"There remaineth therefore a rest to the people of God. For he that is entered into his rest, he also hath ceased from his own works, as God did from his. Let us labour therefore to enter into that rest, lest any man fall after the same example of unbelief" (Hebrews 4:9-11 KJV).

PEACE

Jesus, while on earth, did more than any living man in three and one-half years, yet He was never hurried or never worried. He merely did quickly, gladly, obediently, what God bid Him to do, by the power of the Holy Ghost. Since He was always eager to do His Father's will, there was no friction, no lost motion, no indecision, no fuss or fear or frustration.

It is friction that wears us out, both men and machinery. Oil makes the engine run smoothly, and the "oil of gladness" which only God can furnish, smooths and quiets out the fear, the friction, the fuming and the fussing, and permits God to have His way in our wills, our minds, our spirits, and our bodies. And wherever God is in complete control, there is always complete victory and perfect peace. God is Love and also Health and Power and Peace.

"For he will speak peace unto his people, and to his saints but let them not turn again to folly" (Psalm 85:8 KJV).

GOD'S GOOD FOOD

One more word about food. God made us and He has provided just the right food for our bodies. Just what will make them strong, and keep them strong and well. Our bodies are marvelous miracles, with built-in central heat, air conditioning or cooling, but if we flaunt His wisdom and break His laws of health, we can hardly expect Him to keep us well for long at a time.

The nearer we can get back to God's natural way of doing things, the better off we are in everything. Yet to serve mankind who live in cities, some of us must live in unnatural surroundings. But we can choose to get as much as possible of His good food, good exercise, good fresh air, good sound sleep, and good positive thinking, and His grace will make up for the rest.

To me it is a mockery, almost blasphemy, for a person to come for prayer and expect God to heal them when they are breaking almost all His rules of health. Some smoke, many eat things that positively poison their bodies. Many never exercise or breathe the fresh outdoor air. They drink coffee, tea, "cokes," eat candy, cakes, etc., and then grumble because they "suffer so many afflictions" as though it were God's fault.

It is a wonder that He is as patient and merciful with us as He is. He does want us to be well, but I believe, even more, He wants us to believe and trust His love and wisdom and to obey His Word.

He has put certain conditions on our being healed. In Exodus 23:25, the condition is: *"You shall serve the Lord your God,"* and not your belly nor your own desires.

I pray that the Lord will use this to your good and His glory, and truly "Satisfy your mouth with good things so that your youth is renewed like the eagle's."

J.A.Dennis

- - - - -

I praise God that someone sent that article to me, because I felt it had so many "good things" in it

that ought to be shared with the Body of Christ. As I
looked up and typed out all the scriptures on what
God told us to eat, I was fascinated that even though
I have read all of these scriptures many times, when
you take them out of the Bible and put them all together at one time, it certainly does tell us very
plainly that God gives the "go-ahead" on certain
foods, and says that other foods are "detestable".

Frances

CHAPTER SEVEN

WHAT IS GOOD HEALTH WORTH?

At one of our meetings recently a woman came up who is a diabetic and was complaining about her extreme exhaustion. I had the entire congregation stand and yell "I hate sugar!" hoping to impregnate their minds with the idea that sugar is absolutely not good for anyone. She said, "Do you mean that I can't even have a little piece of pie with ice cream once in a while?" I said, "No," because that little bit of sin(for a diabetic) will lead to bigger sins. Then she put the frosting on our conversation when she said, "But I LIKE sugar!" So did I, but not any more!

Most sinners love sin, but God certainly doesn't. And the same thing is true of those who are bothered with the symptoms of either hypoglycemia or diabetes. They "love" sweet things which are a real disaster area for them.

I want to reach the potential victim of hypoglycemia and diabetes as much as I want to reach the individuals who already know they have a malfunction of the pancreas. Probably the reason for this is that when the pancreas isn't functioning properly, it can cause numerous other symptoms which I personally did not experience, but from reading several books on the subject, I am convinced must be apparent in many cases.

First of all, let me very simply explain what these two diseases are. I am not a doctor, and if there is any question in your mind about whether you are a potential candidate for either diabetes or hypoglycemia, get to your doctor immediately!

I believe one of the reasons God is having me write this book is to help a lot of people out of a false faith which says it's immoral to go to a doctor. I suppose there are those individuals who never run into a problem of any kind that doesn't get healed, but the majority of us don't operate in that realm. Let me say right here, it's no sin to go to a doctor, and don't let anyone put condemnation on you because you do!

Diabetes is simply a case where the pancreas is not supplying or producing insulin for the body. Hypoglycemia is the result of the body producing too much insulin and even though they are opposites, the symptoms are very similar. The person with hypoglycemia is often nervous, irritable, sleepless, tired, edgy, and subject to uncontrollable fits of temper, has difficulties in concentrating, and a completely unjustified feeling that something terrible is about to happen.

Sometimes people with hypoglycemia may be sexually frigid, have nightmares, dizziness, blurred vision and even at times consider suicide. Many times individuals with these symptoms will be put into a class of "hypocondriacs" who do nothing but think about the things that are wrong with them, when their body is simply oversupplying them with insulin.

You will remember when I was in the Atlanta airport I felt exhausted and horrible when I had "overdosed" myself with insulin medication. The hypoglycemic individual, because of eating too much sweets, will also put themselves into an insulin shock, produced by their own body oversupplying their normal needs. I ate candy to bring myself out of insulin shock because the pancreas works when sugar has been eaten so I needed something to offset the problem of too much insulin. The person with low blood sugar makes himself or herself worse by eating sugar because they overstimulate their already overproducing pancreas. In either case, sugar is a killer for both types of individuals.

Often the person with hypoglycemia is considered a neurotic, slightly eccentric, or just a plain nut. Families find it hard at times to sympathize with a person who has had a personality change and they think it is without any apparent cause. Maybe a glucose tolerance test would help in this area.

Even in what is called complete medical check-ups, diabetes or hypoglycemia can be overlooked. I went through one of the best Christian clinics in the United States, and nothing showed up concerning diabetes. It can be missed by the best of doctors and clinics if the glucose tolerance test is not taken.

Statistics show that one out of every four individuals has signs of a tendency toward diabetes. One doctor said that "the low blood sugar of today is the diabetes of tomorrow."

When the pancreas is overactive, as it is in hypoglycemia, it finally gives up from overwork and quits completely, which then throws that person into diabetes.

I know that I have oversimplified trying to explain these two diseases, but I hope I have put enough in to tease your mind enough to get to a doctor to find out the problem in your life if you have one.

Did you know that Americans stimulate the pancreas with a teaspoonful of sugar every 35 minutes, 24 hours a day for a lifetime. That's perhaps enough sugar to exhaust the pancreas and probably cause diabetes. It is certainly enough to overstimulate the gland and throw us all into insulin shock. Isn't that a shocking discovery?

It is not my desire nor my intention to attempt to medically classify anyone, but to bring a message of hope for healing and an encouragement to seek help if you need it and have had any of the symptoms which are mentioned anywhere in this book.

My total desire is to have us all clean up our act, both spiritually and physically. Take a good look at your pantry. How much sugar and sugar products are there? How many cake mixes, how much sugar-coated cereals are there? How many cans of fruit do you have on your shelves that are filled with "heavy syrup"? How many cans of pop do you have that are loaded with caffeine and sugar? How about candy?

How about the cookie jar? Is it full? How about jello? It's approximately 84% sugar. And how about the ice cream and sauces in your refrigerator? All loaded with cocaine (my term for sugar).

I remember hearing someone mention that they ate whole grain cereals without sugar. I thought, "How awful—who could ever eat cereal without a lot of sugar?" I discovered that whole grain cereals are a lot better without sugar than they are with sugar. I am fascinated at the way Charles and I eat all foods without sugar today when formerly we loaded them up!

I believe God has given us (the Body of Christ) a tremendous job to do in these last few years before He returns. We need to be in tip-top health to be able to go when He calls us to go. We shouldn't want to stay at home because we're "tired" or have some other reason.

We need to begin to think intelligently where our health is concerned, and not be ruled by the senses which tell us that we need to have dessert after meals. You can have dessert, but let's make it an apple or a half of a banana. Praise God for refrigeration today so we can have fresh fruit all year long.

I think about what J.A. Dennis said about eating pork, and I remember a few years ago when Charles was working in our office at home. He had just read that "Jesus died for us because He wanted to," and in the stillness of our office, God spoke to him and said, "I don't want you to eat pork any more."

Charles never questioned God because he wanted to please Him. Charles has never eaten pork from that day to this. He knew God knew what was good for him. That could have been a big decision for Charles, because he was a pork lover. He loved bacon, sausage and ham almost better than anything else. When we were traveling on the road, he would order ham and eggs almost every morning for breakfast. He loved "fat back" and beans (and so did I) but we don't eat them any more, because Charles' desire is to please God above all else.

God didn't tell me not to eat pork, but suddenly the desire for anything with pork or ham in it also disappeared from my life. Maybe it was the scripture putting pork and mice in the same category that took the desire right out of me. I don't know what it was, but the desire is gone.

We were recently with D.L. Browning who pastors the Kingsway Cathedral in Des Moines, Iowa, and he said God had dealt with him in the matter of sugar a couple of years ago. At that time he wore a 46 size coat. Today, he wears a 42. He made a tremendous statement to God, "God, I don't have any will power. I have the will and you've got the power, so let's put it together." He said he was instantly delivered of a desire for sugar. Try it!

Charles and I have started taking a vitamin every day. We have many brands in our pantry, but we are especially partial to a Super B Complex vitamin which seems to give some energy but does not increase the appetite. That has always been my problem in the past. Any vitamin would make me want to clean out the refrigerator of anything and everything in it ten times a day! You should experiment until you find the vitamin or vitamins that suit your particular body needs the best.

God just dropped a bombshell in my mind recently where grandchildren are concerned. Bob's and Joan's four little ones have always loved Grandma's pocketbook because they always knew there was something good in it for them. Maybe just a couple of mints, or a bag of candy in our Bible bag to give to them when we got off the plane, but always something that "tickled their palates."

Suddenly I realized what I was doing to my grandchildren whom I love dearly. I was encouraging them to get all "hyped" up on sugar so they couldn't go to sleep at night, creating cavities in their teeth and a possible problem later on in life.

Now they still love Grandma's pocketbook because it always has something in it for them. But it's NOT candy! They met us in the Dallas airport the other day when we had an hour's layover and we got off with a jar of dry roasted peanuts, unsalted, and they had a ball eating them. Nutritious and good, but no sugar! We all must have looked like a bunch of monkeys to anyone who passed by, because each little girl had a handful of peanuts, and so did Grandma and Grandpa!

My son and his family are completely different. A few years ago we were with them on my birthday

and they gave me a box of candy. I opened it and
passed it around for everyone to eat. The four children there said, "No thanks, we don't like candy!"
Praise God, their mother raised them on fruit for
dessert instead of cakes and pies. It shocked me at
the time that they didn't like candy, but today I am
grateful to God that they don't.

Grandmothers, hear the warning from God
about your grandchildren. Let's stop bringing them
"goodies" which are really "baddies" in disguise.
Let's get our children away from what the devil is
trying to do.

A friend of ours shared a problem concerning a
hyper-active child. He had so much energy that it
was impossible for anyone to control him. They
could not discover the cause nor the cure until someone said, "Why don't you take him off of all sugar."
They did, and in a very short time the child was normal. Sugar for our children and grandchildren
comes from the cauldron of the devil himself!

What is good health worth? The devil always
advertises God's goodness by perversion trying to
make the counterfeit look and taste better than the
genuine. We think sweet foods look and taste better
than fruit or vegetables, but because we have destroyed or damaged our taste buds with perverted
foods, the truth is hidden from us. Let's get our taste
buds working normally again! And let's not ruin the
taste buds and health of our grandchildren.

I just reread my book GOD'S ANSWER TO
FAT, and decided it was still the perfect answer, not
only for fat people, people with or without diabetes

or hypoglycemia, but also for the health and alertness of the entire family. Because of the disastrous effects of diabetes in my body, I got discouraged when my weight came back, but praise God, now I know there wasn't anything wrong with GOD'S ANSWER TO FAT. Everything in it is still the answer!

I'm using the guidelines in GOD'S ANSWER TO FAT again. That imperfect pancreas was what threw me off, but praise God I've got a new one and lots of other health blessings besides!

This morning Charles and I had uncooked oatmeal with a few blueberries, two strawberries, four pecans, and a part of a banana cut into it. We used about one-half cup of regular milk, no sugar, and it was delicious! If you had ever told me we'd be eating oatmeal or cereal of any kind without sugar, I would have told you that you were off your rocker. Oatmeal is wholegrain, no sugar added, no additives, natural, fiber, low sodium, no cholesterol and economical besides. Try it, you might be surprised how good it is! The original recipe for "Swiss Oatmeal" appears in the fabulous SKINNIE MINNIE RECIPE BOOK.

I have shared this story from the very depths of my heart with you, because I believe God has a message for the Body of Christ who maybe will hear and believe through the message in this book.

I didn't think it could happen to me, but it did! You may not think it can happen to you, but it can! You don't need to let it happen, because by tempering your appetite where sugar is concerned, you can evade the problems I went through.

My heart is crying out to you to get yourself prepared for the soon return of the Lord Jesus Christ. We can never do it if we have a lack of energy. I wish I was the world's most eloquent writer so that I could convey to you what has happened since God healed me and I went off of sugar completely!

It is almost impossible for me to believe how all of my mental faculties have returned, even sharper than I ever remember. My ability to plow through work is incredible. I can dictate hundreds of letters without ever running out ot Holy Ghost steam! I can write the tabloid plus all the other letters I compose without any difficulty at all. My mind seems to be able to run in fifty directions all at the same time, and yet think clearly on each issue!

Just as cocaine clouds the drug user's mind, I believe sugar does the same thing, only worse. The "high" you get from sugar is a temporary thing, but the payment for it is long-term and just as expensive as cocaine. Sugar should be thrown out of every home, and this includes brown sugar as well! Sugar is sugar, regardless of what color it is.

Remember, I'm not a doctor, so I can't prescribe for you, but I certainly can recommend some good, common sense things. One of them is to visit your doctor if you have any question about your vulnerability to either of these two diseases mentioned in this book. The second is to throw all those desserts out of your life which contain sugar. Next, tell the devil that you HATE sugar!

Lay your hand on the area where your pancreas

lies, and believe with me for a new pancreas for you as you lay the other hand on this book. We've prayed and asked God to so anoint every book that comes off of the press with such Holy Spirit power that flames of fire will shoot out of this book at your pancreas!

Now, you call it into being with us by praying,
"Father, in the name of Jesus, I command a new pancreas in my body. Thank you, Jesus. Praise you, Father!"

P.S. As I proofed the final typesetting copy of this book, God's Holy Spirit nudged me to write a little P.S. so that everyone may receive all the help they need to keep them out of the trap into which I fell.

You may have read this book and thought, "Isn't it awful what Frances had to go through. I praise God that I've never slept for six straight days!"

Mine was an acute case, but something of which I should have been aware of long before. I ignored all the little symptoms completely, probably because the thought of me being a diabetic was the furthest thing from my mind. If anyone had even suggested to me that I was a possible candidate for diabetes, I probably would not have even considered that likelihood.

At this point and time, you perhaps are not where I was, because if you were, you would know

what your problem was. So I want especially to
reach that individual who has just little tiny signs of
a change in the body that might be so slight that you
are not even aware of them. And I want you to catch
the devil at the very start of his attack on you instead of waiting as long as I did before I finally got
smart and realized that something had drastically
gone wrong with my body.

While I do not want to be an alarmist, there are
a few things that stand out in my mind as being the
first evidences of a real problem.

Do you have swelling in your legs? Does your
body retain water? Do your hands feel a little swollen and stiff in the mornings even though they lose
this feeling shortly after you "get going" in the
morning? Do you have a feeling in your legs that
they are heavier than normal? Do you find it difficult to move as quickly as you normally do?

All of these signs were little things that were
present in my body for a long time. The longer some
little symptom stays in your body, the longer it will
take you to recognize that it is abnormal. I had gotten so used to the fact that my body retained fluid
that I never realized it was a "new" thing happening
to me, and had increased in its scope.

I recall that I was aware that there seemed to be
an excessive retention of water, but as the years
went on, I didn't even think about it as something
unusual because it was normal for me to retain
water all the time

The "heaviness" in my legs was an encroach-
ment upon my body that was one of the most dif-

ficult for me to pinpoint when it started. It was an insidious, treacherous problem which came so gradually that I didn't even realize it was there until it was really there!

Do you bounce up from a chair as fast as you formerly did? Do you find it easier to sit in a chair and let someone else get up for you? These were some of the first little signs as I remember them, and I attributed the lack of desire to get up and get something I needed to the fact that I had been on my feet speaking so much that I was just plain tired.

The devil is a liar, and there is not a bit of truth in him, and he will come in sneaky and diverse ways to fool you and keep your eyes off of the real problem. Jesus gave us all power in heaven in earth and He said, *"Behold, I give you the authority to trample on serpents and scorpions, and over all the power of the enemy, and nothing shall by any means hurt you"* (Luke 10:19 NKJV).

Jesus has given us power to stomp the devil right out of our lives, but He expects us not to do the things that play right into the devil's hands. I overheard a diabetic the other night say, "I rebuke the sugar in this ice cream in the name of Jesus and it shall not hurt me!" Foolish, foolish, foolish. Jesus has given us the authority to stomp the devil, but remember it is the devil who wants to get involved with all those gooey messes which do look so superdelicious and taste exactly the same way. They're fabulous! But Jesus gives us the power to overcome the desire for the food of the devil which is the thing that harms us so much!

You can never stomp out the devil when you continue to do the things he wants you to do. As long as you continue to believe that sugar isn't going to hurt you, you are playing right into the devil's hands. He can convince you that you absolutely cannot say "no" to sugar! He can convince you that you do not have the will power to overcome your desire for something sweet, but remember, YOU have MORE power than he does, so just laugh in his face and go eat some blueberries! I finally discovered his evil plot to destroy my body with the sweet things I loved so much and I just quit using his products.

And while we're on the subject of food, let me give you another good hint in this area before I take up the next point and symptom to look for in your own self-analysis to either prepare yourself for a visit to the doctor, or to correct it before you need to seek outside help. You can pray all you want to and ask God to help you, but if you continue to eat the things that are marked as a disaster area, your prayer will go unanswered!

We are subject to advertising wherever we go. Television shows one commercial after the other, and each one is designed to make you immediately run to the store and purchase what they're talking about, or get on the telephone and call some Wats line number to get some product that you will probably never use.

Americans are compulsive buyers and that's why we need to be careful to not fall for all the advertising gimmicks. Snack foods like potato chips and similar foods are a standard part of most lunches. Children love them for "snacks", between meals and we munch on them while drinking cokes and watching T.V. These are some of the worst foods we can eat and yet they're served at almost every luncheon I've attended. Every reception has all kinds of beautiful dips surrounded by potato chips or some similar product.

We've discovered that whole-wheat crackers with no additives are much better tasting than these other little items, and should be used for any kind of a dip you choose, with excellent results.

Caffeine drinks also need to be tossed out the window. Both in coffee and cola drinks, it does nothing but aggravate hypoglycemia and diabetic patients. Even with the sugarless drinks, the caffeine is still present, and probably does as much damage as anything we eat or drink. Good old water is a wonderful substitute for all the other drinks, because so many drinks which are labeled as "juice" have only a little bit of juice, but a tremendous amount of sugar or corn syrup, which is still sugar.

The closer we get to eating and drinking the things as God made them, the better off we will be!

Probably the second area where the devil deals with us even more than the first one is in our minds. Over and over again I have laid hands on individuals who have confessed that their problem is a loss of memory. We laughingly toss it off as "old age" when good memory is a thing that we need to maintain all of our lives.

The most dramatic instant change that I noticed in myself when I ground to a halt on the sugar and

threw it all out the window, was the immediate return of my ability to remember even remote details
which recently seemed to vanish from my mind
when I needed to recall them.

If for no other reason than an experiment, each
of us ought to try giving up sugar for a week or ten
days, just to see how smart we really can be. Keep
it up forever and then we'll realize how smart we
can be since we possess the mind of Christ!

We can get so easily trapped into eating things
that contain sugar if we don't look at the labels.
Most people at some time buy lunch meat for a quick
snack. Did you ever look at the label? Most of them
contain sugar, corn syrup, dextrose or some other
sweetening agent. I looked at a number of them the
other night while I was in the super market, and was
shocked to discover how many of them have these
hidden ingredients in them which we might never
suspect from the taste alone!

Along with the sugar affecting the mind, it
seemed my ability to allow the love of God to flow
through me was hindered by something. Today I can
see that my ability to feel and express love was cur-
tailed until I threw the sugar out. I am not a doctor,
and do not claim to know much about medical
things, but I only know what throwing the sugar out
did to increase my keenness and awareness of emo-
tions in my own life. Everything goes into focus better and everything can be appreciated much more
when sugar is a "has been" in your life.

You must really mean business, or you wouldn't
have gone this far in the book, but if you're having

problems getting the love of sugar out of your life, or if you have any other problems with diabetes or hypoglycemia, please don't hesitate to write to me, so that we can pray for you, or even send you an anointed little prayer cloth to give you some additional Holy Ghost power to overcome your problems and your wrong desires (for sugar). Just to have someone agree with you in prayer can accomplish miracles in your life, and to know that someone is standing in agreement with you often spells the difference between victory and defeat. Not only will Charles and I pray for you, but our entire staff will pray for you until we have chopped off the hands of the devil to make him loose his grip on your body.

Nothing is impossible with God! If we can begin to believe that we actually do have the authority passed on to us by Jesus, and we begin to use it, we can put the devil on the run so fast, he'll never be able to get back to us.

Remember that we are as close to you as your typewriter or your pen and paper. We won't give you any medical advice because we believe if you need that you should go to a qualified physician, but we'll give you all the prayer power you need as we stand in agreement with you.

Write to me.

Frances Hunter
201 McClellan
Kingwood, TX 77339